Information Now

A Graphic Guide to
Student Research
and Web Literacy

SECOND EDITION

MATT UPSON,

HOLLY LUETKENHAUS,

C. MICHAEL HALL,

AND KE~~~ CANNON

D1447497

THE UNIVERSITY OF CHICAGO PRESS
CHICAGO AND LONDON

THE UNIVERSITY OF CHICAGO PRESS, CHICAGO 60637
THE UNIVERSITY OF CHICAGO PRESS, LTD., LONDON
© 2015, 2021 BY THE UNIVERSITY OF CHICAGO
PUBLISHED 2021
PRINTED IN THE UNITED STATES OF AMERICA

30 29 28 27 26 25 24 23 22 21   2 3 4 5

ISBN-13: 978-0-226-76611-9 (PAPER)
ISBN-13: 978-0-226-76625-6 (E-BOOK)
DOI: HTTPS://DOI.ORG/10.7208/CHICAGO/9780226766256.001.0001

LIBRARY OF CONGRESS CATALOGING-IN-PUBLICATION DATA
NAMES: UPSON, MATT, AUTHOR. | LUETKENHAUS, HOLLY, 1985- AUTHOR. | HALL, C. MICHAEL, AUTHOR. |
    CANNON, KEVIN, AUTHOR.
TITLE: INFORMATION NOW : A GRAPHIC GUIDE TO STUDENT RESEARCH AND WEB LITERACY / MATT UPSON,
    HOLLY LUETKENHAUS, C. MICHAEL HALL, AND KEVIN CANNON.
DESCRIPTION: SECOND EDITION. | CHICAGO ; LONDON : THE UNIVERSITY OF CHICAGO PRESS, 2021.
IDENTIFIERS: LCCN 2020037897 | ISBN 9780226766119 (PAPERBACK) | ISBN 9780226766256 (EBOOK)
SUBJECTS: LCSH: INFORMATION LITERACY—COMIC BOOKS, STRIPS, ETC. | INTERNET LITERACY—COMIC
    BOOKS, STRIPS, ETC. | LIBRARY RESEARCH—COMIC BOOKS, STRIPS, ETC. | LCGFT: COMICS (GRAPHIC
    WORKS)
CLASSIFICATION: LCC ZA3075 .U67 2021 | DDC 025.5/24—DC23
LC RECORD AVAILABLE AT HTTPS://LCCN.LOC.GOV/2020037897

CONTENTS

PREFACE

This book has pictures, we swear! You just have to get past this enormous one-page chunk of text before you are rewarded with the ample fruits of your labor. OK, OK, take one quick sneak peek. Turn the page but come right back.

Great. Satisfied? Since we've got you here, let's talk about what we hope to do in this book.

This book is about information. How to find the right kind, how to use it effectively, how to evaluate it efficiently, etc. As a current or perhaps soon-to-be undergraduate, the information you use—and your understanding of it—is critical to your success as a student, future professional, and global citizen. We want this book to transform the way you think about information. We want you to be more critical of the information you find and use. We want you to have a better understanding of where the information you use comes from and how it can affect people in good ways and bad. We want you to be more aware of how to locate the best information for your needs. And we want you to realize that finding the best information can be hard work, especially now that there is more information being created by more people than ever before in human history—and a lot of that information can be confusing, misleading, or intentionally harmful. We want you to do a lot of things, but we're here to help. And when I say "we," I mean librarians. Obviously we're a little biased here, but librarians can be an important part of your quest for information. We know our way around books. That's been our job for quite a while now. But more importantly, we're information experts. Books aren't our only tools; we're not limited to one medium. We know how to find stuff, and we can help you figure out how to find the right stuff on your own. So, if this book teaches you one thing (hopefully, it will teach you more, but . . .), it's that your friendly neighborhood librarian can and should be one of your first stops when you start your research.

All right, we've said enough here. Read the book, learn something new, and enjoy!

INTRODUCTION

WHEW! WELL, NOW THAT **THAT'S** OVER, YOU CAN UNDERSTAND HOW DAUNTING INFORMATION CAN BE.

THINGS CHANGED REALLY QUICKLY THANKS TO THE INTERNET. NOW **BILLIONS** OF PEOPLE CAN CREATE AND DISSEMINATE INFORMATION IN THE BLINK OF AN EYE.

BUT YOU ALREADY KNOW THAT. YOU'VE PROBABLY POSTED SOMETHING ONLINE TODAY YOURSELF, MAKING YOUR OWN THOUGHTS AVAILABLE FOR THE WORLD TO SEE. AND GUESS WHAT?

MILLIONS, EVEN **BILLIONS** OF OTHER INTERNET USERS DID THE SAME THING.

THIS CAN BE GREAT! THE INTERNET HAS MADE IT EASIER FOR PEOPLE IN MARGINALIZED AND UNDER-REPRESENTED GROUPS TO HAVE THEIR VOICES AND STORIES HEARD. AND WITH MORE INFORMATION AVAILABLE, WE CAN BECOME MORE INFORMED, INTELLIGENT, AND RESPONSIBLE GLOBAL CITIZENS.*

*FOR UP-TO-DATE STATISTICS ON WORLDWIDE INTERNET USAGE, SEE THE INTERNATIONAL TELECOM-MUNICATION UNION'S ICT FACTS AND FIGURES PAGE AT http://www.itu.int/en/ITU-D/Statistics/Pages/facts/default.aspx.

BUT SINCE ANYONE CAN DUMP INFORMATION, RELIABLE OR NOT, INTO THE FLOW, WE HAVE TO DEAL WITH AN INCREASING AMOUNT OF INFORMATION POLLUTION.

ALSO, THERE'S OFTEN GREAT INFORMATION HIDDEN BEHIND PAYWALLS, OR SERVICES YOU HAVE TO SUBSCRIBE TO, LIKE A NEWS SERVICE. IF YOU CAN'T PAY FOR ACCESS, YOU MAY NEVER SEE IT.

AND THEN YOU HAVE TO DECIDE WHAT KIND OF INFORMATION IS BEST FOR YOUR PROBLEM OR PROJECT. YOU'LL NEED DIFFERENT INFORMATION FOR WRITING AN ACADEMIC PAPER THAN FOR CHOOSING WHICH MOBILE DEVICE TO BUY.

SO, THAT CONFUSION YOU FEEL ABOUT WHAT'S THE RIGHT RESOURCE TO USE?

THAT'S PART OF INFORMATION OVERLOAD.

AND INFORMATION OVERLOAD ISN'T JUST ABOUT THE HUGE NUMBER OF PEOPLE CREATING INFORMATION EACH DAY. IT'S ABOUT TECHNOLOGY, SPEED, AND ACCESS, TOO.

HEY!

REFERENCE

NOWADAYS, IT IS INCREDIBLY EASY FOR AN INDIVIDUAL TO CREATE AND DUPLICATE INFORMATION.

create and duplicate information
create and duplicate information
create and duplicate information
create and duplicate information

WAY BACK WHEN, STUDENTS WERE FORCED TO USE A CONTRAPTION KNOWN AS A TYPEWRITER, OR EVEN—GASP!—WRITE THINGS OUT BY HAND. CREATING JUST ONE COPY TOOK A **LOT** OF WORK.

...ay before that, scribes labored countless hours to write and illustrate documents by hand. Each copy was unique and valuable, and often available only to a select few, like the nobility who could afford vast libraries.

MOVABLE TYPE WAS INVENTED IN CHINA IN THE ELEVENTH CENTURY AND IN EUROPE A FEW CENTURIES LATER. AND WHEN JOHANNES GUTENBERG DEVELOPED THE PRINTING PRESS IN EUROPE IN THE FIFTEENTH CENTURY, MAKING MULTIPLE AND ACCURATE COPIES OF DOCUMENTS BECAME MUCH EASIER AND FASTER.

I'M SETTING ALL KINDS OF RECORDS HERE!

INFORMATION CREATION STATION

IN FACT, "EASIER AND FASTER" COULD BE THE MOTTO FOR INFORMATION CREATION AND DUPLICATION OVER THE MILLENNIA. IT TOOK A LONG TO TIME TO PICK UP STEAM, BUT NOW THAT IT HAS, THERE SEEMS TO BE NO SLOWING IT DOWN.

INTRODUCTION

THERE ARE ALSO MORE WAYS TO **ACCESS** INFORMATION THAN THERE USED TO BE.

WE USED TO HAVE TO **GO TO** THE INFORMATION IN MANY CASES.

THIS REQUIRED TIME AND MONEY,* WHICH NOT EVERYONE HAS TO SPARE.

*TIME AND MONEY ARE STILL OFTEN REQUIRED TO ACCESS INFORMATION, ESPECIALLY ACADEMIC INFO, BUT IT LOOKS A BIT DIFFERENT NOW. READ ON!

NOW, MORE THAN EVER, THE INFORMATION **COMES TO** US VIA APPS, SOCIAL MEDIA, AND WEBSITES.

BEING CONNECTED TO THE WORLD WIDE WEB HAS BECOME A NECESSITY OF MODERN LIFE. THE INTERNET IS WHERE PEOPLE GO TO SHARE NEWS, FIND AND APPLY FOR JOBS, SHOP, AND COMMUNICATE WITH OTHERS.

IT CAN BE TOO MUCH: TOO MANY WAYS FOR INFORMATION TO REACH US AND NOT ENOUGH WAYS TO FILTER OUT WHAT WE DON'T WANT.

MANAGING ALL OF THE INFORMATION THAT WE COME ACROSS CAN BE A CHALLENGE BECAUSE WE ENCOUNTER SO MUCH OF IT IN SO MANY DIFFERENT WAYS.

I LIKE BOOKS.

AND THE PATHS TO ACCESS ARE STILL MULTIPLYING. WHAT WILL BE THE NEXT NEW WAY TO USE INFORMATION? AUGMENTED REALITY? WIRELESS INTERNET ACCESS POINTS IN OUR BRAINS?

SOUNDS LIKE SCIENCE FICTION, SURE, BUT THE TOOLS WE USE EVERY DAY WOULD SOUND LIKE ALIEN TECHNOLOGY TO THE PEOPLE OF FIFTY, EVEN TWENTY YEARS AGO.

LACKING ACCESS TO THE INTERNET IS A SERIOUS DISADVANTAGE THAT MANY STILL STRUGGLE WITH TODAY. THE NEXT TIME YOU REACH FOR A PHONE OR COMPUTER TO GO ONLINE, THINK ABOUT HOW DIFFERENT YOUR LIFE WOULD BE IF YOU **DIDN'T** HAVE A COMPUTER AT YOUR FINGERTIPS 24/7.

I HAVE NO IDEA WHICH WAY TO TURN!

NO GPS

JOB APPLICATION

Apply Online

NOW THINK ABOUT HOW DIFFICULT IT WAS TO TRANSFER INFORMATION BACK IN THE DAY...

THIS LETTER MUST BE DELIVERED WITH THE UTMOST *HASTE!* LET NOTHING HINDER THE SWIFTNESS OF YOUR STEED, NOR THE FORTITUDE OF YOUR SPIRIT!

YES, MILORD!

THIS MIGHT BE AN EXAGGERATION, BUT YOU GET THE POINT. INFORMATION HASN'T ALWAYS BEEN EASY TO SHARE.

AND BECAUSE OF THAT, MOST INFORMATION THAT WAS SHARED WAS EITHER EXCEPTIONALLY IMPORTANT...

"DUDE! PIZZA 2NITE?"

...OR CAME FROM SOMEONE WITH THE MEANS TO SHARE IT. YOU CAN IMAGINE THAT LEFT A LOT OF PEOPLE OUT OF THE INFORMATION LOOP.

OF COURSE, THERE HAVE ALWAYS BEEN WAYS TO COMMUNICATE EFFICIENTLY WITHOUT ADVANCED TECHNOLOGY. FOR EXAMPLE, THE USE OF SMOKE SIGNALS AND CARRIER PIGEONS ALLOWS FOR THE QUICK TRANSMISSION OF INFORMATION, BUT THAT INFORMATION MAY BE OF LIMITED USE.

CRITICAL THINKING EXERCISES

Before you begin: Make a blog, website, or other social media space, or start a dedicated handwritten notebook as you work through the chapters and exercises in this book. Answer questions or respond to what you're reading using text, images, video, sound, or other media. Make sure that if you're using information or media from somewhere else, you're somehow noting that in your responses. We'll talk about using information ethically later, but for now, you can keep it informal and provide a link to the original source.

1. Is information overload a problem for you? How do you deal with huge amounts of information you encounter in your daily life?

2. Have you ever encountered a website, news article, or other piece of information that required you to sign in, subscribe, or pay a fee to access it? How did you respond? Do you think everyone has the ability to do the same thing you did?

3. Make a list of the different ways in which you have privileged access to information. For example, does your school have a library that can provide books, databases, and news subscriptions? Is it easy and affordable for you to visit a public library? Does your family subscribe to any information sources? Do you have a smartphone and reliable internet? Do you have a computer in your home? What tools or paid access do you have that others might not? Once you have a list, consider this: What would it be like not to have that level of access?

4. We all have limited amounts of time and energy to spend focusing on tasks. How do you prioritize what information you pay attention to online? Where do you choose to spend your limited time and attention? Why do you choose those things?

CHAPTER ONE
THE PROCESS

Steps to Finding and Using the Right Information. Anytime. Anywhere.

NERVOUS YET? DON'T WORRY. WE'RE HERE TO HELP.

IN THIS CHAPTER, WE'LL DISCUSS HOW TO DIVE INTO THAT GIANT MESS OF INFORMATION AND UNEARTH WHAT YOU NEED TO CREATE SOMETHING COHERENT, STRUCTURED, AND USABLE. **RESEARCH** IS THE PROCESS OF SEARCHING FOR, SELECTING, EVALUATING, AND USING INFORMATION.

WE STUDY THE RESEARCH PROCESS MOSTLY FROM A CLASSROOM PERSPECTIVE, BUT YOU CAN APPLY THESE PRINCIPLES **ANY TIME** YOU NEED TO FIND AND USE INFORMATION.

NOT ACCURATE

ha ha!

RESEARCH ISN'T SOMETHING TEACHERS, PROFESSORS, AND LIBRARIANS MAKE YOU DO JUST BECAUSE THEY LIKE SEEING YOU SUFFER...IT'S A SKILL SET THAT'S USEFUL OUTSIDE THE CLASSROOM, IN THE WORKPLACE, AT HOME...EVERYWHERE!

for sale

—WAAAAH!

IMAGINE YOU NEED INFORMATION ON YOUR COMMUNITY'S WATER QUALITY. HOW DO YOU GET IT?

DOES THAT USED CAR YOU'RE LOOKING AT HAVE A GOOD SAFETY RECORD? WONDERING IF YOUR CHILD MIGHT NEED TO SEE A DOCTOR?

HOW DO YOU FIGURE OUT WHAT INFORMATION IS SAFE TO USE?

REGARDLESS OF WHAT APPROACH YOU TAKE, YOU'LL BEGIN WITH AN IDEA, A TOPIC.

PICK SOMETHING YOU'RE INTERESTED IN, SOMETHING YOU HAVE A **QUESTION** ABOUT. IF THE TOPIC IS ASSIGNED OR CHOSEN FOR YOU, APPROACH IT IN A WAY THAT'LL ALLOW YOU TO BE CREATIVE AND FIND THE INTERESTING ASPECTS OF THE TOPIC.

YOU'LL FIND THAT YOUR WORK WILL BE MUCH BETTER IF YOU'RE INTERESTED.

IF THE RESEARCH IS FOR A CLASS, BE SURE TO READ THE DETAILS OF THE ASSIGNMENT, AND ASK YOUR INSTRUCTOR FOR CLARIFICATION IF YOU'RE NOT SURE OF THE ASSIGNMENT'S PURPOSE. THAT PURPOSE WILL GUIDE YOUR RESEARCH.

IF, FOR EXAMPLE, YOU NEED TO WRITE AN ARGUMENT PAPER, YOU'LL HAVE TO FIND INFORMATION THAT ENGAGES WITH RESEARCH AND MULTIPLE PERSPECTIVES.

AND BE SURE TO PLAN AHEAD. YOU MIGHT THINK YOU CAN GET AWAY WITH PUTTING THINGS OFF UNTIL THE LAST MINUTE, BUT THAT **WILL** BACKFIRE EVENTUALLY. YOU CAN NEVER ACCOUNT FOR EVERY POSSIBILITY.

WAIT UNTIL THE LAST MINUTE TO DO YOUR RESEARCH, AND EVENTUALLY THAT "LAST MINUTE" WILL BE THE DAY YOUR INTERNET GOES DOWN, OR THE LIBRARY GETS FUMIGATED, OR YOU BECOME THE FIRST FLU CASE OF THE SEASON.

NO SIGNAL

LIBRARY

CLOSED for FUMIGATION

JEEZ, WHAT ARE THE ODDS?

OK, SORRY FOR THE LECTURE. BACK TO THE...UH...LECTURE. SO, LET'S SAY YOU HAVE YOUR TOPIC, AND YOU'RE READY TO START RESEARCHING—

SEARCH ENGINE ALGORITHMS!

WHOA, HOLD UP.

YEAH, THAT'S A TOPIC...A BIG TOPIC THAT IS STILL EMERGING AND BEING DEBATED EVEN AS IT IS BEING RESEARCHED...

ARE YOU REALLY UP TO SUMMARIZING ALL OF THAT IN TEN PAGES?

chirp.

THAT'S WHAT I THOUGHT. HERE'S WHAT WE'RE GOING TO DO. TAKE THAT TOPIC AND **NARROW IT DOWN.** CHOOSE ONE ASPECT OF YOUR TOPIC AND ASK A QUESTION ABOUT IT.

HMM...OK. ARE SEARCH ENGINE ALGORITHMS BIASED?

THAT'S A GOOD START!

STILL, THE QUESTION'S VERY BROAD, AND IT'S VAGUE. WHAT DO YOU MEAN BY "BIASED," AND HOW DO YOU DETERMINE THAT? ANY PARTICULAR SEARCH ENGINE?

YOU'LL NEED TO CLARIFY YOUR QUESTION BY DIGGING A LITTLE DEEPER. COMING UP WITH A MANAGEABLE QUESTION CAN BE TOUGH WHEN YOU DON'T KNOW THE TOPIC WELL. IF THAT'S THE CASE, SPEAK WITH YOUR INSTRUCTOR OR A LIBRARIAN, OR START WITH SOME GENERAL INFORMATION ON THE TOPIC.

(WE'LL TALK ABOUT HOW TO FIND THAT SOON.)

GO DO THAT. I'LL WAIT HERE.

CRITICAL THINKING EXERCISES

1. Describe or visually depict the process you go through when searching for information. Be creative and consider all the different variables at play. (Here are a few examples: Do you have to be working in a certain location or have your desk organized just so? Do you always start in the same place? Is your process linear, or do you jump around a lot between tasks?)

2. How do you determine what sources of information to look at? What criteria do you use to evaluate information online? (Be specific—don't just say you look for "credible" websites. How do you determine whether something is credible?)

3. Describe a recent time you searched for something online, the steps you went through, and your thought process throughout as you made decisions about where to search, what to click on, etc. It doesn't have to be academic focused; we search for personal information all the time.

4. Next time you have a research assignment, keep a "research log," where you track where you search, what terms you use, what you find, and any other steps you go through. Once you have completed the assignment, reflect back on the experience of keeping the log, whether it was helpful, and what you learned about your own research process as you worked.

NOW THAT YOU'VE HAD TIME TO CHIP AWAY AT THAT QUESTION, WHAT DO YOU HAVE FOR ME?

MY RESEARCH QUESTION IS "DO ALGORITHMS MAKE RACISM AND SEXISM WORSE?"

EXCELLENT! STILL A BIT BROAD, BUT GETTING THERE. TRY NARROWING IT DOWN SOME MORE. YOU CAN EVEN SHIFT THE FOCUS OF THE TOPIC IF YOU THINK IT MIGHT LEAD YOU IN A USEFUL DIRECTION.

OH.

HOW ABOUT "DO ALGORITHMS REINFORCE AND AMPLIFY ISSUES OF RACISM AND SEXISM IN SEARCH ENGINE RESULTS?"

"ALGORITHMS CAN REINFORCE AND AMPLIFY ISSUES OF RACISM AND SEXISM IN SEARCH ENGINE RESULTS."*

THAT'S A GREAT QUESTION! NOW, SINCE THIS IS A RESEARCH PAPER, TURN THAT QUESTION INTO A STATEMENT.

GREAT! THAT'S WHAT WE CALL YOUR "THESIS STATEMENT."

YOU'VE TAKEN A STAND ON THE TOPIC, AND NOW IT'S YOUR JOB TO GATHER EVIDENCE TO SEE IF YOU'RE CORRECT.

SOMETIMES YOU'LL FIND EVIDENCE THAT PROVES YOUR THESIS WRONG. DON'T IGNORE THAT EVIDENCE! YOU CAN ADJUST AND REFINE YOUR THESIS AS YOU COLLECT AND ANALYZE A VARIETY OF SOURCES. BE FLEXIBLE AND OPEN TO SURPRISING FINDINGS WHILE STILL LOOKING AT THINGS WITH A CRITICAL EYE. THAT SHOWS YOU'VE GROWN AS A RESEARCHER.

DETOUR AHEAD: FOLLOW THE RESEARCH

*FOR MORE FASCINATING AND IMPORTANT INFORMATION ON MACHINE BIAS AND ALGORITHMS, SEE CHAPTER 5.

CHAPTER ONE

YOU NOW HAVE A TOPIC AND A STRONG QUESTION TO GUIDE YOUR RESEARCH. BUT WHERE DO YOU START?

A GOOD PLACE TO BEGIN IS WITH SOME BACKGROUND INFORMATION. MANY LIBRARIES HAVE ENCYCLOPEDIAS. THESE COVER **LOTS** OF TOPICS AND PROVIDE ENOUGH INFORMATION TO HELP YOU IDENTIFY **KEYWORDS**, OR TERMS YOU CAN USE LATER ON IN YOUR IN-DEPTH SEARCHING.

NOW, SOME INSTRUCTORS AND LIBRARIANS MIGHT SAY GOOGLE AND WIKIPEDIA ARE COMPLETELY OFF-LIMITS, BUT I DISAGREE.

THAT DOES **NOT** MEAN YOU SHOULD JUST DO A QUICK SEARCH WITH GOOGLE, COPY THE INFORMATION FROM WIKIPEDIA, AND SLAP YOUR NAME ON THE PAPER. THAT'S NOT COOL AT ALL.

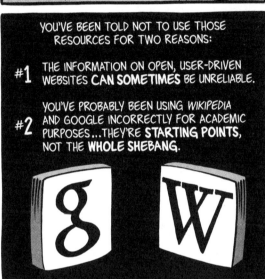

YOU'VE BEEN TOLD NOT TO USE THOSE RESOURCES FOR TWO REASONS:

#1 THE INFORMATION ON OPEN, USER-DRIVEN WEBSITES **CAN SOMETIMES** BE UNRELIABLE.

#2 YOU'VE PROBABLY BEEN USING WIKIPEDIA AND GOOGLE INCORRECTLY FOR ACADEMIC PURPOSES...THEY'RE **STARTING POINTS**, NOT THE **WHOLE SHEBANG**.

GOOGLE IS GREAT FOR SEARCHING FOR BACKGROUND INFORMATION AND PROVIDING SOME CONTEXT.

THE PROBLEM IS THAT IT GIVES YOU A LOT OF RESULTS TO SEARCH THROUGH, AND YOU HAVE TO BE GREAT AT IDENTIFYING WHAT IS LEGIT AND WHAT ISN'T. WE'LL LEARN HOW TO DO THIS LATER IN THE BOOK.

WIKIPEDIA IS PRETTY USEFUL AS YOUR FIRST EXPOSURE TO A TOPIC, BUT IT CAN BE UPDATED AND EDITED BY JUST ABOUT ANYONE. THIS CAN BE A REAL PROBLEM, ESPECIALLY WITH CONTROVERSIAL SUBJECTS. SOMETIMES PEOPLE TRY TO PROMOTE THEIR OWN VIEWPOINTS ON A TOPIC, AND THE FACTS GET BURIED UNDER BIASED OPINION!

THE WORLD'S BANKS ARE SECRETLY CONTROLLED BY **INTERDIMENSIONAL ALIENS!**

EVEN THOUGH *WIKIPEDIA* EDITORS TRY TO MAKE SURE EDITS ARE AS ACCURATE AND UNBIASED AS POSSIBLE, YOU SHOULDN'T USE IT AS A DIRECT SOURCE.

INSTEAD, USE IT TO GUIDE YOU TO OTHER, MORE RELIABLE RESOURCES. EVEN *WIKIPEDIA* SAYS THAT'S WHAT YOU SHOULD DO.*

AGAIN, WE'LL DISCUSS THIS MORE LATER ON.

*SEE en.wikipedia.org/wiki/ Wikipedia:Researching_with_Wikipedia.

ANOTHER EXCELLENT SOURCE OF INFORMATION: JOURNAL ARTICLES. JOURNALS (IN THIS CASE) AREN'T DIARIES CONTAINING SOMEONE'S PRIVATE THOUGHTS. WE'RE TALKING ABOUT ACADEMIC JOURNALS.

NOT ACCURATE

DEAR DIARY: TODAY, I AM TOTALLY FILLING YOU WITH EASILY CROSS-REFERENCED RESEARCH TOPICS!

AN **ACADEMIC JOURNAL ARTICLE** IS A SHORTER DOCUMENT WRITTEN AND REVIEWED BY PROFESSIONALS IN A SPECIFIC FIELD, LIKE MEDICINE, EDUCATION, OR ENGINEERING. ACADEMIC JOURNALS ARE FULL OF ARTICLES FOR OTHER PROFESSIONALS ABOUT RECENT RESEARCH IN THAT FIELD.

ASSUMING WE SURVIVE TO WRITE IT, THE ARTICLE ABOUT THIS PROJECT IS GOING TO BE AWESOME.

JOURNAL ARTICLES MAY GO THROUGH AN EXTENSIVE **PEER-REVIEW** PROCESS TO MAKE SURE THEY'RE ACCURATE AND RELIABLE. COMPARED TO BOOKS, JOURNAL ARTICLES CAN BE VERY FOCUSED ON A NARROW SLIVER OF A TOPIC THAT MIGHT SHED SOME LIGHT ON YOUR OWN QUESTION.

HOW NARROW? HOW ABOUT THE SOCIAL IMPLICATIONS OF SINGING IN BARBERSHOP QUARTETS!*

*YEP, THAT'S A REAL ARTICLE: L. Garnett, "Ethics and Aesthetics: The Social Theory of Barbershop Harmony," Popular Music 18, no. 1 (January 1999): 41-61.

SO WHERE DO YOU FIND JOURNAL ARTICLES? THERE ARE A FEW PLACES YOU SHOULD LOOK. FIRST OF ALL, YOUR LIBRARY WILL PROBABLY HAVE SOME PRINT COPIES OF JOURNALS. YOU CAN EITHER BROWSE THROUGH THEM OR USE SOMETHING CALLED AN INDEX TO FIND A PARTICULAR ARTICLE ON A PARTICULAR TOPIC.

OOH, I HAVEN'T READ THIS ONE YET!

BEARDED LIBRARIAN MONTHLY

USUALLY, THE BETTER OPTION IS TO SEARCH WITHIN SOMETHING CALLED A **DATABASE**.

A LIBRARY DATABASE IS A BIG ONLINE WAREHOUSE FULL OF JOURNAL ARTICLES. THEY'RE EASY TO SEARCH AND WORK JUST LIKE A LIBRARY SEARCH, EXCEPT THEY'RE FULL OF INFORMATION ABOUT ARTICLES. MUCH OF THE TIME, YOU CAN DOWNLOAD AN ENTIRE ARTICLE AND NOT WORRY ABOUT FINDING THE JOURNAL ON THE SHELF.

Fun to look at! But won't get you where you need to go.

Useful, relevant, ...and exactly what you need.

MOST OF THE TIME, WITH THE ACADEMIC JOURNAL ARTICLES AND BOOKS FOUND THROUGH THE LIBRARY, YOU'RE GETTING HIGH-QUALITY RESOURCES. STILL, SOMETHING IRRELEVANT CAN SLIP PAST EVERY ONCE IN A WHILE.

WHEN YOU RESEARCH ON THE INTERNET, THE LIKELIHOOD OF STUMBLING ON UNSUITABLE RESOURCES IS GREATER. AND SOMETIMES THE IRRELEVANT STUFF IS WHAT GETS PUSHED AT YOU FIRST.

AGAIN, NOT ALL INFORMATION FOUND ON THE OPEN WEB IS BAD. YOU JUST HAVE TO BE GOOD AT FIGURING OUT WHAT IS APPROPRIATE FOR YOUR NEEDS. PROFESSIONAL RESEARCHERS SOMETIMES TWEET OR BLOG THEIR OWN OPINIONS AND RESEARCH. INFORMATION DOES NOT HAVE TO BE FOUND IN A BOOK OR A FANCY ACADEMIC JOURNAL TO BE VALID AND USEFUL.

MY LATEST RESEARCH CONCLUSIVELY PROVES THAT ELBOW PATCHES ON TWEED JACKETS WORN BY PROFESSORS SIGNIFICANTLY IMPROVE STUDENT ENGAGEMENT, ATTENTION, AND SUCCESS IN THE ACADEMIC CLASS... WAIT, 280-CHARACTER LIMIT... OK... **GOT THAT TWEED, Y'ALL!!!!!!**

snap!

GUESS WHO JUST DEVELOPED A **SWEET** PIEZOELECTRIC ROBOTIC ENDOSCOPE FOR COLONOSCOPY PROCEDURES? THIS GIRL!

TO ARM YOURSELF AGAINST IRRELEVANT, INACCURATE, AND SOMETIMES INSIDIOUS INFORMATION ONLINE, YOU'LL WANT TO KEEP A FEW THINGS IN MIND.

YOU NEED TO KNOW WHO IS RESPONSIBLE FOR THAT INFORMATION.

WHO? WHAT? WHY?

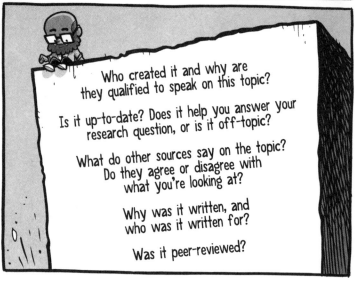

Who created it and why are they qualified to speak on this topic?

Is it up-to-date? Does it help you answer your research question, or is it off-topic?

What do other sources say on the topic? Do they agree or disagree with what you're looking at?

Why was it written, and who was it written for?

Was it peer-reviewed?

SINCE WE JUST DISCUSSED WHAT DEFINES GOOD, RELIABLE INFORMATION, LET'S TOUCH ON **CITATION**. CITATION IS A METHOD USED TO IDENTIFY THE RESOURCES THAT AN AUTHOR HAS USED TO PERFORM THEIR RESEARCH.

YOU'RE GOING TO BASE YOUR WORK ON RESEARCH OTHER PEOPLE HAVE ALREADY DONE. THIS SHOWS THAT YOU KNOW WHAT RELATED WORK HAS BEEN DONE IN THE PAST AND THAT YOUR WORK BUILDS ON IT. YOU'LL FIND BOOKS, JOURNAL ARTICLES, AND OTHER RESOURCES; SYNTHESIZE AND ANALYZE THEM; AND USE THEM AS THE BASIS FOR YOUR OWN CONCLUSIONS.

AND SO YOU HAVE TO CITE THEM.

CITATION IS A NECESSITY FOR A COUPLE OF REASONS. FIRST, THE PEOPLE WHO DID THE WORK BEFORE YOU WANT AND NEED CREDIT FOR THE WORK THEY'VE DONE. YOU WOULDN'T WANT SOMEONE TO RUN OFF AND CLAIM THE WORK YOU'VE DONE AS THEIR OWN, RIGHT? CITATION IS THE **BEST** WAY TO ACKNOWLEDGE THE WORK THAT OTHERS HAVE DONE.

YOUR ARTICLE IS WICKED GOOD, YO.

JUST WRITE A PROPER CITATION, ALREADY!

HUG!

SECOND, READERS NEED TO BE ABLE TO RETRACE YOUR STEPS AND SEE IF THE CONCLUSIONS YOU REACHED ARE JUSTIFIED.

FOR EXAMPLE, ARE THERE OBJECTIVE RESOURCES THAT SUPPORT THE CLAIM THAT YOUR PARENTS HAVE THE WORST TASTE IN MUSIC EVER?

HEY!

YOUR READERS WANT TO SEE HOW YOU CAME TO THAT CONCLUSION BASED ON THE RESOURCES YOU USED. A CITATION IS JUST A WAY TO SAY:

"HEY, I USED THIS RESOURCE, AND YOU CAN FIND IT HERE!"

FINALLY, REMEMBER TO KEEP TRACK OF WHAT YOU FIND AND WHERE YOU FIND IT. DISTRACTIONS HAPPEN!

MY CITATIONS, NOTES, AND HOPES OF FINISHING THIS PAPER

MY TIME AND ATTENTION

OLD MEMES FROM 2017

BE SURE TO RECORD THE SEARCH TERMS YOU'RE USING. AS WE'LL SEE, MINOR CHANGES IN THOSE TERMS CAN COMPLETELY ALTER YOUR SEARCH RESULTS. NOTE WHAT IS SUCCESSFUL AND WHAT DOESN'T WORK.

COPY AND PASTE THE CITATION INFORMATION OF BOOKS, ARTICLES, WEBSITES, AND OTHER RESOURCES INTO A DOCUMENT OR AN EMAIL OR USE THE CITATION GENERATORS AVAILABLE IN LIBRARY SEARCHES AND DATABASES.

YOU CAN ALSO USE FREE OR SCHOOL-PROVIDED CITATION MANAGEMENT SOFTWARE* TO TRACK ALL THE RESOURCES YOU FIND. KEEP AN ONGOING LIST OF WHAT YOU'VE FOUND, WHAT YOU'VE LOOKED AT, AND WHAT YOUR THOUGHTS ARE ON EACH RESOURCE. THIS CAN SAVE A LOT OF TIME AND HASSLE.

*ZOTERO, ENDNOTE, AND REFWORKS ARE JUST A FEW EXAMPLES.

NOW THAT YOU HAVE AN IDEA OF WHAT THE RESEARCH PROCESS IS LIKE, LET'S TAKE A CLOSER LOOK AT HOW INFORMATION IS ORGANIZED, BOTH IN THE LIBRARY WORLD AND ONLINE. ONCE WE HAVE AN IDEA OF HOW IT'S STRUCTURED, WE CAN DO A BETTER JOB OF FINDING THE INFORMATION WE NEED.

PULL!

CHAPTER ONE

CRITICAL THINKING EXERCISES

REMEMBER TO USE YOUR ONLINE TOOL TO RECORD
YOUR RESPONSES TO THE QUESTIONS.

1. Create a concept map for your topic or research question. This will help you visualize all the different aspects of your topic, figure out what you already know about a topic, and identify areas for further research. Here's an example:

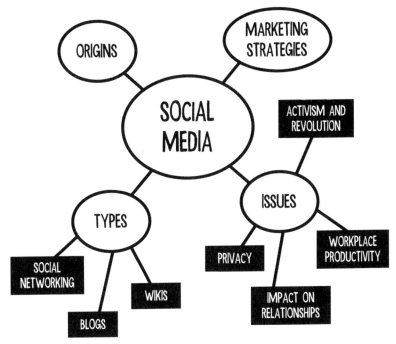

2. When you need to learn the basics about a topic or question, where do you start? (Be honest; it is okay if you use *Wikipedia*, or if you ask a trusted friend or family member!) What do you like about using that source? What are some of the disadvantages of using that source?

3. Do an online search on your topic and find (1) a blog, (2) a professional website, and (3) a public forum. (If you don't know how to find one of those, try adding the type of source you want as a search term along with your topic.) Compare the information you find in each of these different sources. What are the advantages and disadvantages of each source?

CHAPTER TWO
HOW INFORMATION IS ORGANIZED AND FOUND
The Basics

FOR THIS DISCUSSION, I'M HANDING YOU OVER TO ANOTHER LIBRARIAN. SHE'S AN EXPERT IN THE ORGANIZATION OF INFORMATION AND FINDING THE RIGHT RESOURCES.

HI! I HEAR YOU'RE STARTING YOUR RESEARCH SOON! BUT FIRST, LET'S TALK ABOUT HOW INFORMATION CAN BE ORGANIZED, SO WE CAN FIND OUR WAY AROUND THE LIBRARY'S RESOURCES.

SEE YOU LATER!

YOU'RE GOING TO BE USING A LOT OF DIGITAL RESOURCES—AND WE'LL DISCUSS THAT SOON—BUT YOU NEED TO UNDERSTAND THE BASICS OF HOW LIBRARIES ARE TYPICALLY ORGANIZED.

OBVIOUSLY, WE HAVE A SHELF FULL OF BOOKS HERE, BUT HOW ARE THEY ARRANGED? RANDOMLY? BY SUBJECT OR TOPIC, KIND OF LIKE A BOOKSTORE? WELL, SINCE LIBRARIES CAN HAVE LITERALLY TONS OF BOOKS, WE KEEP THINGS AS STRUCTURED AND ORGANIZED AS POSSIBLE, SO FINDING MATERIALS IS EASY.

GEOLOGY

FOSSIL   VOLCANO   CRYSTAL

CLASSIFICATION IS THE METHOD WE USE TO KEEP OUR COLLECTIONS ORGANIZED. EACH ITEM IS DESIGNATED AS PART OF A SPECIFIC SUBJECT GROUP AND THEN A SUBGROUP. FOR EXAMPLE, MOST OF THE BOOKS ON GEOLOGY WOULD BE GROUPED TOGETHER. WITHIN THAT GROUP WE FIND SUBGROUPS, LIKE PALEONTOLOGY, VOLCANOLOGY, AND MINERALOGY.

WHEN YOU SEARCH THE LIBRARY FOR PHYSICAL MATERIALS, YOU'LL SEE A **CALL NUMBER** FOR EACH ITEM. THAT'S JUST AN ALPHANUMERIC* TAG BASED ON THE ITEM'S SUBJECT. IT HELPS ORGANIZE SIMILAR ITEMS TOGETHER AND TELLS YOU WHERE TO LOOK FOR BOOKS. IT'S LIKE THE ADDRESS OF THE ITEM.

"VOLCANOES" 551.21 B891v

*THAT'S A FANCY WAY OF SAYING "LETTERS AND NUMBERS." BUT YOU KNEW THAT.

SCHOOLS AND COLLEGES IN THE UNITED STATES USE TWO MAIN CLASSIFICATION SYSTEMS: THE **DEWEY DECIMAL CLASSIFICATION (DDC)** SYSTEM AND THE **LIBRARY OF CONGRESS CLASSIFICATION (LCC)** SYSTEM.

DEWEY IS MORE COMMON IN PUBLIC AND SCHOOL LIBRARIES, WHILE LCC IS FOUND PRIMARILY IN RESEARCH AND ACADEMIC LIBRARIES.*

*THIS IS GENERALLY TRUE. THERE ARE PLENTY OF EXCEPTIONS, THOUGH.

CHAPTER TWO

> EACH GROUP IS BROKEN DOWN INTO TEN MORE GROUPS, AND EACH OF THOSE TEN GROUPS IS BROKEN DOWN EVEN FURTHER, AND SO ON—THAT'S HOW WE CAN ATTEMPT TO SLOT ALL THE INFORMATION INTO THE APPROPRIATE PLACE.

TECHNOLOGY (600s)

600-609 GENERAL

610-619 MEDICINE & HEALTH

620-629 ENGINEERING

630-639 AGRICULTURE

640-649 HOME & FAMILY MANAGEMENT

650-659 MANAGEMENT & PUBLIC RELATIONS

660-669 CHEMICAL ENGINEERING

670-679 MANUFACTURING

680-689 MANUFACTURE for SPECIFIC USES

690-699 BUILDING & CONSTRUCTION

> ADDITIONALLY, DEWEY NARROWS IT DOWN USING NUMBERS AFTER THE DECIMAL POINT. FOR EXAMPLE, THE CALL NUMBER 339.22 MIGHT DEAL WITH INCOME INEQUALITY, WHILE 339.42 DEALS WITH COST OF LIVING. LET'S LOOK AT EACH PART OF THIS, BECAUSE EACH NUMBER AND EACH PLACE VALUE CARRIES SIGNIFICANCE.

300s Social Sciences

330s Economics

339 Macroeconomics, Wealth

339.2 Distribution of income

339.22 Income inequality

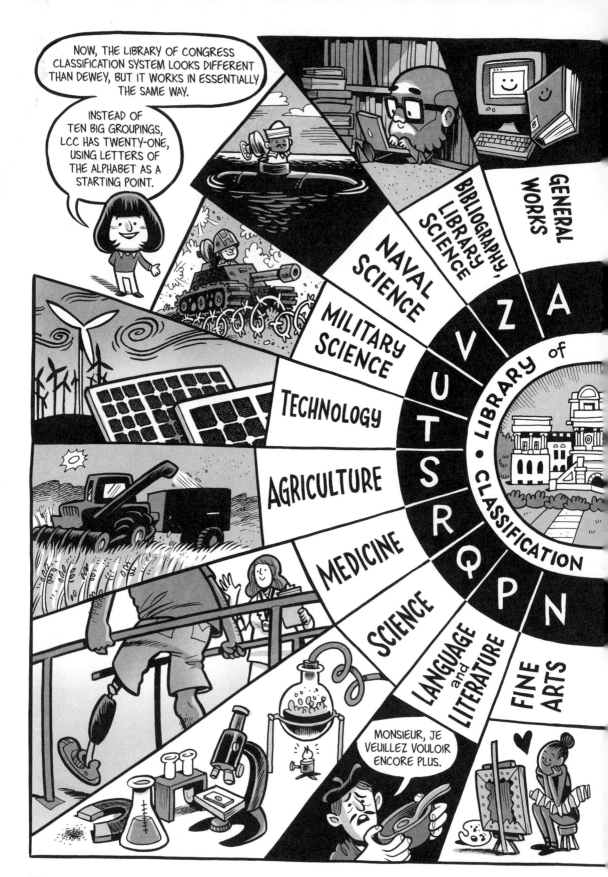

LCC BREAKS TOPICS DOWN WITHIN EACH LETTER, DIVIDING EACH LETTERED "CLASS" INTO "SUBCLASSES."

FOR INSTANCE, IN THIS BREAKDOWN, WE SEE THAT ITEMS ON SCULPTURE ARE FOUND UNDER NB, AND ITEMS ON PAINTING ARE FOUND UNDER ND.

CLASS N — FINE ARTS

SUBCLASS N — VISUAL ARTS

NA	ARCHITECTURE
NB	SCULPTURE
NC	DRAWING, DESIGN, ILLUSTRATION
ND	PAINTING
NE	PRINT MEDIA
NK	DECORATIVE ARTS
NX	ARTS IN GENERAL

FINALLY, LCC INSERTS A NUMBER AFTER THE CLASS/SUBCLASS TO CONTINUE TO NARROW THE FOCUS. BOOKS ON **VARMINT HUNTING*** CAN BE FOUND UNDER SK336.

CLASS S	AGRICULTURE
SUBCLASS SK	HUNTING SPORTS
SK336	VARMINT HUNTING

*AN ACTUAL TOPIC!

SOME LIBRARIES THROW IN A FEW NUMBERS AND LETTERS OF THEIR OWN AFTER THE "OFFICIAL" CALL NUMBER.*

THESE NUMBERS VARY BY LIBRARY AND CAN BE USED TO DESIGNATE THE TITLE, AUTHOR, OR PUBLICATION DATE OF THE BOOK...SOMETIMES EVEN ALL THREE. THIS IS JUST ANOTHER WAY TO REFINE CLASSIFICATION AND PROVIDE A UNIQUE CALL NUMBER FOR EVERY ITEM.

Varmint Hunting by Load N. Mygun

LCC

SK336	M373	v	1998
Call #	Author Last Name Code	First Letter of Title	Year of Publication

DDC

973.52	S337	w	2004

War of 1812 by Touch E. Subject

*THESE ARE ONLY EXAMPLES—YOUR LIBRARY MAY DIFFER.

320.973014 P253p 2012

THE REAL **WEAKNESS** OF THESE CLASSIFICATION SYSTEMS IS THAT WHEN NEW IDEAS COME ALONG OR SOCIAL UNDERSTANDINGS OF OLD IDEAS CHANGE, THE SYSTEMS ARE NOT VERY QUICK TO ADAPT. FOR EXAMPLE, IT WAS ONLY IN 1996 THAT THE TOPIC OF HOMOSEXUALITY WAS CLASSIFIED UNDER "SEXUAL RELATIONS" AS OPPOSED TO "MENTAL DERANGEMENTS" OR "SOCIAL PROBLEMS."

THESE CLASSIFICATION SYSTEMS ORIGINATED IN THE UNITED STATES, SO THEY'RE ALSO BIASED TOWARD AMERICAN AND WESTERN IDEAS. NOT AS MUCH SPACE WAS ASSIGNED TO NON-WESTERN MATERIALS, AND SO THEY MAY NOT BE REPRESENTED EFFICIENTLY.

NOW, ALL OF THAT TALK ABOUT HOW INFORMATION IS ORGANIZED IS PRETTY USELESS WITHOUT AN EFFECTIVE WAY TO SEARCH FOR THAT INFORMATION. BROWSING, WHETHER ON THE INTERNET OR IN PERSON, IS NOT THE MOST EFFICIENT WAY TO FIND EXACTLY WHAT YOU NEED. WHILE IT CAN SOMETIMES BE VERY SERENDIPITOUS, IT CAN ALSO BE UNFOCUSED AND HAPHAZARD.

TO MAXIMIZE THE USEFULNESS OF INFORMATION, WE NEED TO MAKE SURE YOU CAN FIND IT ON PURPOSE, NOT JUST HOPE YOU STUMBLE ACROSS IT BY BLIND LUCK.

MAYBE A COUPLE MORE LEFT TURNS...?

SO HERE COMES **METADATA** TO SAVE THE DAY!

METADATA IS INFORMATION ABOUT... INFORMATION. YEAH, IT'S THAT NERDY.

METADATA HELPS DESCRIBE THE INFORMATION IN A WAY THAT'S EASILY SEARCHABLE BY SYSTEMS LIKE DATABASES AND LIBRARY SEARCHES.

METADATA CAN GET COMPLICATED, BUT HERE'S A SIMPLE EXAMPLE TO SHOW YOU HOW IT WORKS. HERE'S SOME INFORMATION ABOUT A CAR. EACH BIT OF INFORMATION MEANS SOMETHING, SO WE CAN DESCRIBE EACH PART WITH A LABEL.

METADATA ENABLES US TO PUT A SIGN ON A BIT OF INFORMATION EXPLAINING WHAT IT IS. THAT MIGHT NOT BE A BIG DEAL WHEN YOU'RE LOOKING AT JUST ONE ITEM, BUT WHEN YOU WANT TO SEARCH THROUGH HUNDREDS OR THOUSANDS OF RECORDS AND YOU WANT RESULTS THAT MEET ONLY CERTAIN CONDITIONS—CARS WITH UNDER 100,000 MILES OR UNDER $10,000—METADATA IS VITAL!

For sale:
2013 Talambro Lava, 84K, 4D, AC, CD, automatic, $8,250

For sale:
Model Year: 2013
Manufacturer: Talambro
Model: Lava
Mileage: 84,000 miles
# of doors: 4
Air-conditioning: yes
CD player: yes
Transmission type: automatic
Asking price: $8,250

WITHOUT ANY METADATA, OR WITHOUT A CONSISTENT SET OF METADATA, PERFORMING A GENERAL SEARCH OF THE WEB CAN RESULT IN A JUMBLE OF RESOURCES THAT CAN BE CONFUSING, MISLEADING, OR INCOMPLETE.

SEARCH RESULTS:

SOME METADATA WOULD'VE SPARED US THIS **INDIGNITY!**

ALTHOUGH GOOGLE HAS ADVANCED SEARCH OPTIONS, MANY SITES LACK THE METADATA FOR SUCH SEARCHES. BESIDES, THE VAST MAJORITY OF US STILL JUST DO A GOOD OLD-FASHIONED, TRADITIONAL GOOGLE SEARCH ANYWAY... WE GO TO GOOGLE AND JUST START TYPING WHAT WE WANT OR HOPE TO FIND.

WHAT HAS BEEN SEEN CANNOT BE UNSEEN...

DUDE, WE HAVE **GOT** TO LEARN BETTER SEARCH TECHNIQUES.

A GENERAL SEARCH ESSENTIALLY LOOKS FOR YOUR SEARCH TERMS (OR KEYWORDS) WITHIN WEB PAGES RANKED BY GOOGLE. FOR EACH RESULT, THE PAGE IS RANKED ON WHERE AND HOW OFTEN THE PAGE USES A TERM, HOW MANY LINKS IT HAS, AND HOW LONG IT'S BEEN AROUND.*

CAN'T... STOP... LOOKING...

*THERE'S MORE TO IT, BUT THAT'S THE BASIC IDEA.

A GENERAL GOOGLE SEARCH IS LIKE GOING TO A GARAGE SALE AND RUMMAGING THROUGH BOXES FILLED AND LABELED IN A VERY GENERAL WAY. YOU MIGHT FIND A FEW GEMS HIDDEN IN THE BAGS AND BOXES, BUT THERE'LL ALSO BE LOTS OF IRRELEVANT OR USELESS MATERIAL.

YOUR FINDINGS IMPROVE DRAMATICALLY WHEN YOU LEARN HOW TO SEARCH MORE EFFECTIVELY, AND IF THE INFORMATION IS DESCRIBED WITH A CONSISTENT SET OF METADATA!

BABY STUFF

DATABASES AND LIBRARY SEARCHES (WHICH ARE DESCRIBED IN MORE DETAIL LATER) ARE ONLINE LIBRARY RESOURCES THAT USE METADATA TO HELP MAKE SEARCHING EASY.

IMAGINE A HOUSE. THAT HOUSE IS LIKE A LIBRARY DATABASE: IT CAN STORE ITEMS, JUST LIKE DATABASES STORE INFORMATION.

100 DATABASE PLACE

INSIDE THIS HOUSE, EVERYTHING IS WELL ORGANIZED AND LABELED, JUST LIKE A LIBRARY DATABASE.

PING AR

GARDEN HOSES

AU TO PA RTS

OLS

FERTILIZER

AIR PUMPS

OVES

BIKE

AGS

THESE LABELS ARE LIKE METADATA, DESCRIBING THE CONTENTS OF EACH CABINET.

HAND TOOLS

IN A LIBRARY RESOURCE, YOU WOULD SEE SOMETHING LIKE THIS. THIS IS ALL METADATA DESCRIBING A PARTICULAR ITEM. EACH LABEL REPRESENTS A DIFFERENT CHARACTERISTIC OF THAT ITEM.

PRINT   CITE   EMAIL   SHARE

LIBRARY SEARCH

Title: *Evil Geniuses and the Superheroes Who Thwart Them: An Oral History*

Author: L. Luthor

Pages: 326 pages

Publisher: MetropoPress

Publication Date: 1940

Call #: 364.973 L884e

Subject Headings: Organized Crime—United States—History; Criminals; Superheroes; Crime—Prevention

Summary: For years, superheroes have prevented the dawn of a new age, an age dedicated to the consolidation of power under a few magnificent geniuses who have been unjustly labeled as "evil" or "mad." For the first time, the stories of these brave and unique "deviants" are offered in their own words.

IT'S USEFUL TO KNOW THAT INFORMATION IN A DATABASE CAN BE LABELED, BUT IT'S IMPORTANT TO MAKE SURE IT'S LABELED IN A CONSISTENT, STANDARDIZED WAY.

WE WANT THE SAME TYPE OF INFORMATION LABELED THE SAME WAY. IN OUR GARAGE, WE DON'T LABEL ONE DRAWER "POWER TOOLS" AND ANOTHER "ELECTRIC TOOLS." THEY'RE THE SAME THING! WE SHOULD GIVE THEM ONE "OFFICIAL" LABEL AND PUT THEM IN THE SAME DRAWER, EVEN IF MORE THAN ONE LABEL EXISTS.

Looking for ELECTRIC TOOLS? *Try the...* POWER TOOLS DRAWER!

POWER TOOLS

NOW, WE STILL WANT TO MAKE SURE THAT EVEN IF YOU USE THE "WRONG" TERM, YOU CAN GET TO THE RIGHT STUFF. SOMETIMES A NICE LINK CAN SEND YOU TO THE RIGHT PLACE, BUT OFTEN YOU'LL NEED TO TRY DIFFERENT TERMS ON YOUR OWN OR USE THE LIBRARY SYSTEM TO FIGURE OUT WHAT "CONTROLLED VOCABULARY" THEY'RE USING.

WHEN WE ASSIGN ONE STANDARD LABEL TO A SET OF SIMILAR ITEMS, WE CALL THAT A **CONTROLLED VOCABULARY.** IT'S CONTROLLED IN THE SENSE THAT SOMEONE MAKES A DECISION TO FAVOR ONE LABEL OVER OTHERS.

THIS ALSO MEANS THAT **BIASED** SYSTEMS MAY APPLY LABELS THAT ARE OUTDATED, INACCURATE, OR OFFENSIVE.

FLICKS · MOVIES · FEATURE · SCRE... · MOTION PICTURE · FILM · CI...EMA · MOVI...G · ...LMS

FOR EXAMPLE, IN 2016 THE LIBRARY OF CONGRESS PROPOSED CHANGING THE SUBJECT HEADING "ILLEGAL ALIENS" TO "NONCITIZENS" AND "UNAUTHORIZED IMMIGRATION" IN ORDER TO MORE ACCURATELY "DESCRIBE RESOURCES ABOUT PEOPLE WHO ILLEGALLY RESIDE IN A COUNTRY."*

THE US HOUSE OF REPRESENTATIVES VOTED TO RETAIN THE ORIGINAL HEADING SINCE THAT TERM IS USED IN FEDERAL LAW. THIS IS JUST ONE RECENT EXAMPLE OF HOW THE WORDS WE USE TO ORGANIZE AND DESCRIBE INFORMATION HAVE AN IMPACT, NOT ONLY ON HOW WE FIND THAT INFORMATION, BUT ON HOW HUMAN BEINGS ARE REPRESENTED.

DOES THE SYSTEM ACCURATELY REFLECT SOCIETY OR DOES IT LEAVE SOME OUT?

SEE https://www.loc.gov/catdir/cpso/illegal-aliens-decision.pdf.

SEAT OR CHAIR?

SUBJECT HEADINGS ARE A PARTICULARLY USEFUL KIND OF METADATA. REMEMBER THE CONTROLLED VOCABULARY WE JUST DISCUSSED? WELL, IN THIS CASE, THE SUBJECT HEADING IS "CHAIRS." IT COULD HAVE BEEN "SEATS," BUT OUR CATALOGER DECIDED THAT "CHAIRS" IS THE OFFICIAL TERM TO USE.

IF YOU SEARCHED FOR "SEATS," YOU MIGHT SEE A MESSAGE LIKE "SEATS—SEE CHAIRS," WHICH LETS YOU KNOW YOUR TERM IS NOT THE PREFERRED OPTION WITHIN THE SYSTEM. LIBRARY RESOURCES ARE PICKY; IT CAN BE TOUGH TO FIGURE OUT HOW THEY WANT YOU TO SEARCH.

WE ALSO USE SUBJECT TERMS TO INDICATE BOTH BROADER AND NARROWER SETS OF INFORMATION. IN THIS CASE, A BROADER SEARCH TERM WOULD BE "FURNITURE," ENCOMPASSING NOT ONLY CHAIRS, BUT BEDS, SOFAS, TABLES, DESKS, AND SO ON.

BROADER TERM: FURNITURE

SUBHEAD A	CHAIR
SUBHEAD B	BED
SUBHEAD C	SOFA
SUBHEAD D	TABLE
SUBHEAD E	DESK

CHAIRS

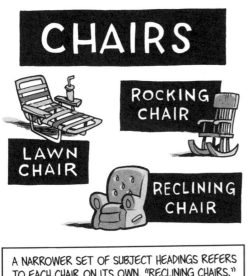

LAWN CHAIR

ROCKING CHAIR

RECLINING CHAIR

A NARROWER SET OF SUBJECT HEADINGS REFERS TO EACH CHAIR ON ITS OWN. "RECLINING CHAIRS," "LAWN CHAIRS," AND "ROCKING CHAIRS" ARE ALL NARROWER TERMS THAN JUST "CHAIRS." ADDITIONALLY, ITEMS CAN FIT INTO MULTIPLE CATEGORIES. A LAWN CHAIR MIGHT BE FOUND UNDER "CHAIRS" AND "OUTDOOR FURNITURE."

SO, WE CAN SEE THAT SUBJECT HEADINGS (WHICH WE'LL USE MORE LATER) ARE BOTH METADATA (A DESCRIPTIVE LABEL) AND A CONTROLLED VOCABULARY (A WAY TO MAKE THAT LABEL **THE** ONE-AND-ONLY OFFICIAL LABEL).

SORRY ABOUT ALL THE PARENTHESES.

METADATA AND CONTROLLED VOCABULARIES MAKE INFORMATION EASIER TO FIND AND PLAY A BIG ROLE IN HOW INFORMATION IS SEARCHED. WHEN THIS LEVEL OF ORGANIZATION IS LACKING, WE CAN HAVE TROUBLE FINDING WHAT WE NEED.

WEBSITES DON'T NECESSARILY HAVE THE SAME RIGOROUS LEVEL OF METADATA THAT A LIBRARY RESOURCE HAS. THERE'S NOT THE SAME LEVEL OF CONSISTENCY AND STANDARDIZATION ON THE OPEN WEB. THIS **POTENTIALLY** MAKES THINGS MORE DIFFICULT TO FIND WITH A GENERAL GOOGLE SEARCH.

Google HQ

SINCE SUBJECT HEADINGS AND SIMILAR METADATA STANDARDS ARE LACKING AND UNEVEN ACROSS THE WEB, GOOGLE AND OTHER SEARCH ENGINES APPROACH SEARCHING DIFFERENTLY. FIRST OF ALL, GOOGLE SENDS OUT DIGITAL "CRAWLERS" OR "BOTS" THAT SCOUT WEBSITES AND REPORT BACK WITH INFORMATION ABOUT THOSE WEBSITES. REALLY, THEY JUST MAKE COPIES AND KEEP TRACK OF LINKS ON A WEBSITE, AND SEND THE INFO BACK TO GOOGLE. (THIS IS ALL **WAY** MORE COMPLICATED THAN I'M MAKING IT SOUND.)

WHEN YOU DO A SEARCH, GOOGLE TAKES THE TERMS YOU USED AND SCANS THEIR ENTIRE STOCKPILE OF INFORMATION ON ALL THESE WEBSITES. IF YOUR TERMS ARE FOUND IN A WEBSITE, THAT WEBSITE GETS LISTED AMONG YOUR RESULTS.

BUT THERE'S SO MANY!

KANSAS CITY BBQ JOINTS

YOUR RESULTS ARE DISPLAYED BASED ON A RANKING SYSTEM THAT GOOGLE KEEPS PRETTY SECRET.* BUT WE DO KNOW THAT THE RANKING IS INFLUENCED BY A COMBINATION OF WHAT GOOGLE KNOWS ABOUT YOU (LIKE YOUR LOCATION AND SEARCH HISTORY), HOW MANY OTHER SITES ARE LINKED TO A PAGE, AND THE "QUALITY" OF THE WEB PAGES DOING THE LINKING.

GOOGLE ASSUMES THAT POPULARITY CAN (IN SOME PART) ENSURE QUALITY, WHICH IS DEBATABLE.

BEST WEBSITES

I WANT TO LINK TO YOU!

*SEE "How Google Search Works" (https://www.google.com/search/howsearchworks/).

CRITICAL THINKING EXERCISES

1. Which library classification systems are you familiar with (if any)? What are some of the benefits and problems with these classification systems?

2. What are some flaws you can identify in library organization systems? How could these systems be improved?

3. Search for books in your library's search system. (Ask for help if you need it.) Evaluate the different call numbers for your results. How similar are they? How different? How do you explain the differences between the various call numbers you see?

4. Find an item in your library search that is relevant to your research topic, and click on it to find more information. This is what we call an item "record." What details (metadata) are provided about the item? Which parts are most useful, and why?

5. Perform a Google search for your topic. Compare this to a library search on your topic. How many results did you get for each? Try looking past the first page of results. What happens as you go deeper into the results from each system?

CHAPTER THREE
SEARCHING FOR LIBRARY RESOURCES
Understanding the Hunt for Information

SO, WHERE DO WE FIND THAT INFORMATION "GOLD"? WELL, FOR ACADEMIC PURPOSES, LIBRARY RESOURCES TYPICALLY PROVIDE THE BEST "GOOD" STUFF TO "BAD" STUFF RATIO. A LIBRARY SEARCH OR DATABASE LISTS ITEMS THAT MAY BE OF HIGHER QUALITY THAN MUCH OF WHAT WE'D FIND ONLINE, SO WE WADE THROUGH LESS GARBAGE.

OPEN WEB

LIBRARY RESOURCES

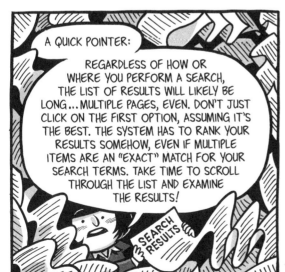

A QUICK POINTER:

REGARDLESS OF HOW OR WHERE YOU PERFORM A SEARCH, THE LIST OF RESULTS WILL LIKELY BE LONG...MULTIPLE PAGES, EVEN. DON'T JUST CLICK ON THE FIRST OPTION, ASSUMING IT'S THE BEST. THE SYSTEM HAS TO RANK YOUR RESULTS SOMEHOW, EVEN IF MULTIPLE ITEMS ARE AN "EXACT" MATCH FOR YOUR SEARCH TERMS. TAKE TIME TO SCROLL THROUGH THE LIST AND EXAMINE THE RESULTS!

SEARCH RESULTS

OBVIOUSLY, IT'S NOT LIKE THE RIGHT INFORMATION WILL JUST FALL IN YOUR LAP. YOU HAVE TO DO SOME WORK. YOU HAVE TO SEARCH.

BUT BEFORE YOU TRY OUT YOUR SEARCH SKILLS, I WANT TO EXPLAIN WHAT A **LIBRARY SEARCH** IS.

Title
Search Statements
Truncati
Boolean Subje t Ter
Opera Author
Breadcrumb Limi
Trail

DOING A LIBRARY SEARCH ALLOWS YOU TO LOOK THROUGH AN ONLINE LIST OF MANY OF OUR RESOURCES. WE MAINTAIN RECORDS OF ITEMS FILLED WITH META-DATA, WHICH ALLOWS US TO SEARCH FOR AND FIND WHAT YOU'RE LOOKING FOR.

BACK IN THE OLD DAYS, BEFORE E-BOOKS AND OTHER DIGITAL RESOURCES REALLY TOOK OFF, A CATALOG WAS A LIST OF ALL THE **PRINT** ITEMS IN THE LIBRARY. AND BEFORE DIGITAL SYSTEMS, THE CATALOG WAS JUST A SYSTEM OF PAPER CARDS ORGANIZED BY TITLE, AUTHOR, OR SUBJECT (METADATA!). SEARCHING WAS A VERY TIME-CONSUMING PROCESS BACK THEN.*

*IT CAN BE NOW, TOO, BUT FOR DIFFERENT REASONS.

REMEMBER THAT THE METADATA IS WHAT WILL BE EXAMINED DURING A SEARCH. THIS "RECORD" CONTAINING THE METADATA (TITLE, AUTHOR, AND SUBJECT, FOR INSTANCE) IS ACTUALLY WHAT THE SYSTEM SEARCHES WHEN WE ENTER OUR TERMS.

MOST PEOPLE DON'T USE THE TERM "CATALOG" TO DESCRIBE LIBRARY SEARCH SYSTEMS ANYMORE.

MOST LIBRARIES NOW USE WHAT ARE CALLED "DISCOVERY SYSTEMS" (WHAT WE'RE CALLING "LIBRARY SEARCH") THAT LIST NOT ONLY THE PHYSICAL ITEMS IN THE LIBRARY BUT ALSO DIGITAL ITEMS LIKE E-BOOKS AND WEBSITES. EACH SYSTEM CAN BE DIFFERENT, BUT MANY OF THE FEATURES AND FUNCTIONS ARE PRETTY STANDARD, AND YOU CAN SEARCH MOST USING THE SAME STRATEGIES.

Title: *Evil Geniuses and the Superheroes Who Thwart Them: An Oral History*

Author: L. Luthor

Pages: 326 pages

Availability: Central Library 2nd Floor and one e-book: *Click Here for e-Book*

Publisher: MetropoPress

Publication Date: 1940

Call #: 364.973 L884e

ISBN #: 978-X-368-44531-X

Subject Headings: Organized Crime—United States—History; Criminals; Superheroes; Crime—Prevention

Contents: Chapter titles include "Faster than a Speeding Meanie Pants," "Able to Destroy My Evil Plans in a Single Bound," "Criminals Are a Brave and Intelligent Lot," "With Great Power Comes Great Inability to Understand the Overarching Grand Design of My 'Schemes'"

Summary: For years, superheroes have prevented the dawn of a new age, an age dedicated to the consolidation of power under a few magnificent geniuses who have been unjustly labeled as "evil" or "mad." For the first time, the stories of these brave and unique "deviants" are offered in their own words.

Preview This Book link | Help | Cite/Export | Print | Email | Save | Share links

CHAPTER THREE

SINCE THERE'S SO MUCH INFORMATION TO SEARCH THROUGH, GOOD **SEARCH TERMS** ARE KEY TO LOCATING THE BEST INFORMATION.

EARLIER, WE TOUCHED ON HOW TO DEVELOP A RESEARCH QUESTION OR THESIS STATEMENT. NOW WE'LL BREAK A THESIS STATEMENT DOWN INTO USABLE SEARCH TERMS. LIBRARY SEARCHES AND DATABASES WON'T LET YOU TYPE A QUESTION INTO THE SEARCH BAR LIKE GOOGLE DOES (AND EVEN GOOGLE DISCOURAGES THAT PRACTICE). WE WANT TO CHIP OFF THE USELESS INFORMATION AND FIND THE HEART OF THE THESIS STATEMENT.

JUST THE BASICS.

Social media enables political organizing but can also make activists more vulnerable to harassment.

IN THIS THESIS STATEMENT, WE CAN IDENTIFY A FEW KEY PARTS AND GET RID OF THE EXTRA VERBIAGE.

Social media enables — TIKTOK, TWITTER, SOCIAL NETWORKS
political organizing but can — POLITICS, DISSENT, RALLY
also make activists more — PROTESTER, DISSENTER, RESISTANCE
vulnerable to harassment. — THREATS, DOXING

ONCE YOU HAVE YOUR KEY TERMS OR CONCEPTS, IT IS USEFUL TO COME UP WITH SOME SYNONYMS OR RELATED TERMS.

REMEMBER, YOUR INITIAL TERMS MIGHT NOT BE THE ONLY APPLICABLE TERMS USED, SO WE WANT TO MAKE SURE WE ACCOUNT FOR MULTIPLE OPTIONS.

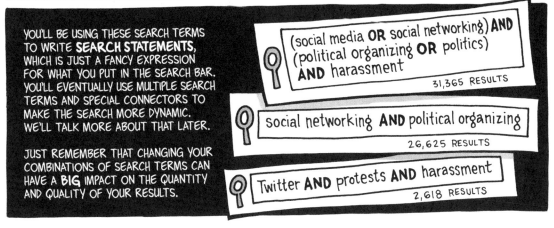

YOU'LL BE USING THESE SEARCH TERMS TO WRITE **SEARCH STATEMENTS**, WHICH IS JUST A FANCY EXPRESSION FOR WHAT YOU PUT IN THE SEARCH BAR. YOU'LL EVENTUALLY USE MULTIPLE SEARCH TERMS AND SPECIAL CONNECTORS TO MAKE THE SEARCH MORE DYNAMIC. WE'LL TALK MORE ABOUT THAT LATER.

JUST REMEMBER THAT CHANGING YOUR COMBINATIONS OF SEARCH TERMS CAN HAVE A **BIG** IMPACT ON THE QUANTITY AND QUALITY OF YOUR RESULTS.

(social media **OR** social networking) **AND** (political organizing **OR** politics) **AND** harassment
31,365 RESULTS

social networking **AND** political organizing
26,625 RESULTS

Twitter **AND** protests **AND** harassment
2,618 RESULTS

BE SURE TO WRITE DOWN YOUR SEARCH TERMS TO KEEP TRACK OF ALL THE DIFFERENT WAYS YOU SEARCH. SOME WORDS WORK BETTER THAN OTHERS, SO YOU'LL WANT TO NOTE WHICH ONES WORK, WHICH ONES DON'T, AND IF ANY PARTICULAR COMBINATION GIVES YOU BETTER RESULTS.

NOW LET'S TALK ABOUT THE VARIOUS TYPES OF SEARCHES AND SOME TOOLS YOU CAN USE TO HELP MAKE YOUR SEARCH TERMS AS FLEXIBLE AND USABLE AS POSSIBLE.

THE MOST BASIC TYPE OF SEARCH IS A **KEYWORD SEARCH.** KEYWORD SEARCHES WILL GIVE YOU A BROAD SET OF RESULTS AND ARE USUALLY SET UP AS THE DEFAULT SEARCH OPTION IN MANY DATABASES.

Databases:
- UltraCat
- Academic World Search Plus

🔍 comic books **AND** culture

Results: 4 of 120

 1. *Global Comics*, by Pierre Martin; publisher: PAU Press, 2016

 2. *Comics Crisis!*, by Jackson P. Forte; publisher: Pivot Press, 2013

 3. *Cartoon Art and World War II*, by Dr. Emily Rickens; publisher: University of Greenstead Press, 2018

 4. *Female Superheroes: Cultural and Social Influences*, by Mary Zeitner; publisher: Booth & Saffer, 2020

LET'S SAY YOU'RE LOOKING FOR INFORMATION ON KING JAMES OF ENGLAND (AND SCOTLAND). YOU TYPE "KING JAMES" AND PERFORM A KEYWORD SEARCH. MANY OF YOUR RESULTS WILL BE EXACTLY WHAT YOU'RE LOOKING FOR, BUT THERE WILL ALSO BE SOME STUFF THAT'S COMPLETELY IRRELEVANT.

- *King James Bible: A New History*, by Suzanne Middleton. New York: Smyth & Willingham, 2008. Location: 1st Floor. Call # 220.5203 M533k
- *The Lion King* (video recording). Location: Children's DVDs. Call # DVD Lion King
- *King James: LeBron on the Court*, by Martin Zale. Los Angeles: Tooth & Nail Sports, 2020. Location: Children's Browsing Room. Call # 796.323 James 2009
- *A Far and Lonely Land: A Novel*, by James King. Minneapolis: Bound for Glory, 2000. Location: Browsing Room. Call # 813 K564f 2000

WE GOT THESE RESULTS BECAUSE A **KEYWORD** SEARCH LOOKS AT MOST OF THE METADATA IN A RECORD. KEYWORD SEARCHING DOESN'T DISTINGUISH BETWEEN SEARCHES FOR A TITLE, AUTHOR, SUBJECT, OR SOMETHING ELSE ENTIRELY.

IT ALSO DOESN'T NECESSARILY FIND YOUR SEARCH TERMS RIGHT NEXT TO EACH OTHER. THAT'S WHY WE GOT *THE LION KING* (FEATURING THE VOICE OF **JAMES** EARL JONES), AND A BOOK ON LEBRON JAMES, WHOSE NICKNAME IS "KING JAMES." AND FINALLY, WE ALSO FOUND A BOOK BY AN AUTHOR NAMED JAMES KING. SOME OF THESE RESULTS ARE USEFUL, BUT IRRELEVANT ONES ARE MIXED IN. THAT'S THE WAY A GENERAL KEYWORD SEARCH WORKS.

CHAPTER THREE

A KEYWORD SEARCH IS LIKE WALKING INTO OUR TRUSTY GARAGE HERE AND SAYING, "I NEED SOMETHING TO HELP ME DO YARD WORK," THEN SEARCHING THROUGH EACH DRAWER TO FIND EVERYTHING WITH ANY CONNECTION TO YARD WORK.

YOU'LL FIND SOME STUFF THAT FITS, AND YOU'LL FIND SOME STUFF THAT COULD WORK BUT ISN'T QUITE RIGHT, AND YOU'LL FIND A LOT OF STUFF THAT JUST WON'T WORK. YOU'VE SEARCHED THROUGH EVERYTHING, BUT YOU DIDN'T USE THE EXISTING ORGANIZATION TO FOCUS YOUR SEARCH.

U Search [🔍_____] Advanced Search

U Search *ADVANCED SEARCH*

All Fields ▾
• FULL TEXT
• SUBJECT
• AUTHOR
• TITLE
• CALL NUMBER
• SERIES TITLE
• JOURNAL TITLE

[_____] AND ▾
[_____] AND ▾
[_____] AND ▾

DATES: [____] TO [____]

DON'T WORRY, THOUGH— WE CAN STEP UP TO AN **ADVANCED SEARCH.** YOU CAN USUALLY FIND A LINK CALLED "ADVANCED SEARCH" OR A DROP-DOWN MENU ALLOWING FOR MORE SEARCH OPTIONS. SELECT WHAT TYPE OF ADVANCED SEARCH YOU'D LIKE TO PERFORM. WE'LL TRY A SUBJECT SEARCH FIRST.

AS WE DISCUSSED PREVIOUSLY, CONTROLLED VOCABULARIES HELP US ORGANIZE INFORMATION BY USING A STANDARD LABEL FOR SIMILAR ITEMS. SUBJECT HEADINGS OR SUBJECT TERMS, WHICH ARE A TYPE OF CONTROLLED VOCABULARY, CAN ALSO HELP US **FIND** INFORMATION.

SEARCH RESULTS:

TITLE: *Evil Genius*
AUTHOR: L. Luthor
SUBJECT HEADINGS:
Organized Crime— United States—History; Criminals; Superheroes; Crime— Prevention

WHEN I PERFORM A **SUBJECT SEARCH,** THE SYSTEM LOOKS THROUGH A LIST OF SPECIFIC LABELS ASSIGNED TO ITEMS, THEN PROVIDES ME WITH A LIST OF ITEMS MATCHING THAT LABEL. UNLIKE A KEYWORD SEARCH, A SUBJECT SEARCH JUST LOOKS THROUGH THE METADATA ASSOCIATED WITH SUBJECT TERMS, NOT THE **WHOLE** RECORD.

🌐 ACADEMIC WORLD SEARCH PLUS

[comic books] [SUBJECT TERMS ▾]

CHOOSE THIS OPTION TO JUST LOOK AT SUBJECT HEADINGS

• "Article Title"
Author Last Name, First Name. *Journal Title* volume #, issue # (Date): page range.
Subjects: **Comic books**, strips, etc.; Motion pictures and **comic books**

• "Article Title"
Author Last Name, First Name. *Journal Title* volume #, issue # (Date): page range.
Subjects: **Comic books**, strips, etc.; Horror **comic books**, strips, etc.

LET'S GO BACK TO THE GARAGE. A **SUBJECT SEARCH** IS MUCH NEATER AND TIDIER THAN A KEYWORD SEARCH. IMAGINE THAT EACH DRAWER REQUIRES A KEY TO OPEN. THE RIGHT SUBJECT TERM ACTS AS THE KEY TO A SPECIFIC DRAWER: IT LETS US SELECT THE CORRECT ITEMS FROM A FOCUSED SET OF RESOURCES.

MANY ITEMS HAVE MORE THAN ONE SUBJECT TERM ASSOCIATED WITH THEM. FOR EXAMPLE, THIS SET OF ELECTRIC GARDEN SHEARS CAN BE LOCATED IN THE DRAWER FOR "GARDEN TOOLS" AND THE DRAWER FOR "POWER TOOLS." IT FITS INTO BOTH CATEGORIES AND CAN BE FOUND WITH A SEARCH FOR EITHER.

BUT WHAT IF YOU'RE UNFAMILIAR WITH THE CORRECT SUBJECT HEADING FOR A TOPIC? THERE ARE A FEW OPTIONS TO GET ON THE RIGHT TRACK. USE A THESAURUS TO COME UP WITH ALTERNATE TERMS THAT MIGHT BROADEN OR NARROW YOUR SEARCH. OR USE A SUBJECT-TERM GUIDE PROVIDED IN THE SEARCH SYSTEM, AND CHECK THE OFFICIAL SUBJECT TERM.

🔍 tools

Broader terms: ☐ HARDWARE
Narrower terms: ☐ AXES
　　　　　　　 ☐ HAMMERS
　　　　　　　 ☐ PLIERS
　　　　　　　 ☐ SCREWDRIVERS
Related terms: ☐ EQUIPMENT

Title: *Evil Geniuses and the Superheroes Who Thwart Them: An Oral History*

Author: L. Luthor

Pages: 326 pages

Publisher: MetropoPress

Publication Date: 1940

Call #: 364.973 L884e

Subject Headings: Organiz̲e̲d̲ ̲U̲nited States—History; Criminals; Superheroes; Crime̲ ̲Prevention

Summary: For years, superheroes have prevented the dawn of a new age, an age dedicated to the consolidation of power under a few magnificent geniuses who have been unjustly labeled as "evil" or "mad." For the first time, the stories of these brave and unique "deviants" are offered in their own words.

CLICK HERE FOR ALL "SUPERHERO" RESOURCES IN ONE PLACE!

IF YOU'VE ALREADY FOUND A USEFUL ITEM THROUGH A KEYWORD SEARCH, LOOK AT THE SUBJECT TERMS LISTED IN THAT RECORD, THEN CLICK ON THE ONE THAT BEST MATCHES YOUR SEARCH. THAT'LL TAKE YOU TO A WHOLE LIST OF ITEMS MATCHING THAT SUBJECT HEADING!

AND REMEMBER THAT PEOPLE OR EVEN FICTIONAL CHARACTERS CAN BE **SUBJECTS**, TOO.

WHILE A SINGLE-TERM KEYWORD SEARCH CAN BE TOO VAGUE, WE CAN USE SOMETHING CALLED **BOOLEAN OPERATORS** TO ENTER **MULTIPLE** SEARCH TERMS AND MAKE A REALLY **GOOD** KEYWORD SEARCH.

BUT BEFORE WE DEFINE BOOLEAN OPERATORS, LET'S DESCRIBE KEYWORD SEARCHES IN A NEW WAY.

LET'S SAY WE WANT TO RESEARCH THE OLD PIRATE SHIPS, SO WE PERFORM A KEYWORD SEARCH FOR "PIRATES." THIS CIRCLE REPRESENTS EVERY SINGLE ITEM IN THE LIBRARY WITH THE WORD "PIRATES" IN ITS RECORD. AS YOU CAN SEE, IT'S WAY TOO BROAD.

NOW IMAGINE ANOTHER CIRCLE REPRESENTING A SECOND KEYWORD SEARCH: "SHIPS." THESE TWO CIRCLES REPRESENT DIFFERENT SEARCHES AND DIFFERENT RESULTS. BUT THIS SEARCH HAS THE SAME PROBLEM… IT'S TOO BROAD.

PIRATES

SHIPS

BUT WHAT IF WE DID A SEARCH FOR BOTH KEYWORDS AT THE SAME TIME? WE'D GET A NARROWER RANGE OF RESULTS CONSISTING ONLY OF ITEMS WHOSE RECORDS CONTAIN THE KEYWORDS FROM BOTH CIRCLES. OUR SEARCH IS MORE FOCUSED. IT'S STILL NOT QUITE THERE YET, THOUGH… WE AREN'T LOOKING FOR INFORMATION ON MODERN PIRATE SHIPS.

PIRATES  SHIPS

BY ADDING ONE MORE SEARCH TERM, "HISTORY," WE GET **ANOTHER** GROUP OF ITEMS ADDED TO THE SEARCH. BY ADDING A SEARCH FOR "HISTORY," I HAVE ALMOST GUARANTEED THAT I WILL GET A RESULTS LIST FULL OF ITEMS ABOUT PIRATE SHIPS…THE OLD-SCHOOL HISTORICAL KIND WE'RE INTERESTED IN!

YO-HO, ME HEARTIES!

HISTORY

PIRATES

SHIPS

BOOLEAN OPERATORS MAKE THAT KIND OF SEARCHING POSSIBLE. THEY ALLOW YOU TO NARROW OR BROADEN A SEARCH BY USING THREE WORDS:

AND: *Narrows*

OR: *Broadens*

NOT: *Narrows*

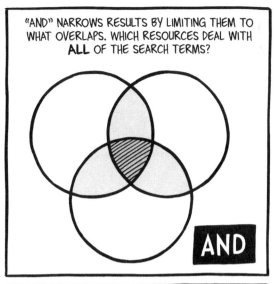

"AND" NARROWS RESULTS BY LIMITING THEM TO WHAT OVERLAPS. WHICH RESOURCES DEAL WITH **ALL** OF THE SEARCH TERMS?

AND

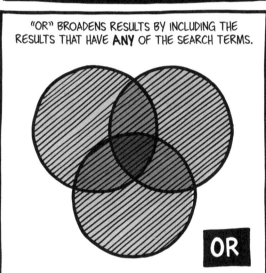

"OR" BROADENS RESULTS BY INCLUDING THE RESULTS THAT HAVE **ANY** OF THE SEARCH TERMS.

OR

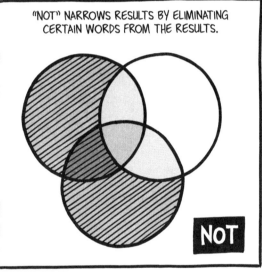

"NOT" NARROWS RESULTS BY ELIMINATING CERTAIN WORDS FROM THE RESULTS.

NOT

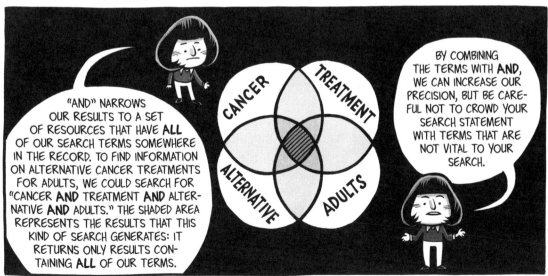

"AND" NARROWS OUR RESULTS TO A SET OF RESOURCES THAT HAVE **ALL** OF OUR SEARCH TERMS SOMEWHERE IN THE RECORD. TO FIND INFORMATION ON ALTERNATIVE CANCER TREATMENTS FOR ADULTS, WE COULD SEARCH FOR "CANCER **AND** TREATMENT **AND** ALTERNATIVE **AND** ADULTS." THE SHADED AREA REPRESENTS THE RESULTS THAT THIS KIND OF SEARCH GENERATES: IT RETURNS ONLY RESULTS CONTAINING **ALL** OF OUR TERMS.

CANCER TREATMENT ALTERNATIVE ADULTS

BY COMBINING THE TERMS WITH **AND**, WE CAN INCREASE OUR PRECISION, BUT BE CAREFUL NOT TO CROWD YOUR SEARCH STATEMENT WITH TERMS THAT ARE NOT VITAL TO YOUR SEARCH.

"OR" BROADENS A SEARCH BY LOOKING AT SEARCH TERMS ON EITHER SIDE OF THE OPERATOR. TO FIND INFORMATION ON "GENETICALLY MODIFIED FOOD" WHILE INCLUDING ALTERNATE, RELATED TERMS LIKE "GMO"* AND "GENETICALLY ENGINEERED FOOD," WE USE **OR** TO SEARCH FOR EVERY ITEM THAT HAS **ANY** OF THOSE WORDS IN THE RECORD. USE **OR** WHEN YOU WANT TO INCLUDE TERMS THAT HAVE SIMILAR MEANING (SYNONYMS) IN YOUR SEARCH RESULTS.

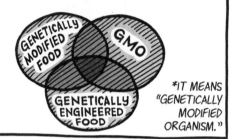

*IT MEANS "GENETICALLY MODIFIED ORGANISM."

"NOT" LIMITS OUR SEARCH BY EXCLUDING A WORD OR PHRASE.* TO LOOK FOR INFORMATION ON GENETICALLY MODIFIED FOOD OUTSIDE THE UNITED STATES, FOR EXAMPLE, SEARCH FOR "GENETICALLY MODIFIED FOOD **NOT** UNITED STATES." THIS EXCLUDES ANY RESULTS THAT MENTION THE UNITED STATES.

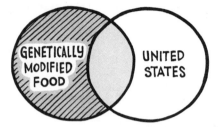

***NOT** CAN ELIMINATE USEFUL INFORMATION, AS WELL, SO USE IT CAREFULLY!

ADVANCED SEARCH:

🔍 bananas

AND ▾ pie

AND ▾ recipe

NOT ▾ pecans

IF YOUR SEARCH SYSTEM OFFERS AN "ADVANCED SEARCH" OPTION, USE IT! ADVANCED SEARCHES OFTEN OFFER MULTIPLE SEARCH BARS SO YOU CAN ENTER EACH OF YOUR TERMS SEPARATELY AND SELECT YOUR OPERATOR (**AND, OR, NOT**) FROM A DROP-DOWN MENU.

GENETICALLY MODIFIED FOOD
GENETICALLY ENGINEERED FOOD
FOOD SAFETY

FINALLY, WE CAN USE PARENTHESES TO HELP ORGANIZE A COMPLICATED SEARCH STATEMENT. THIS IS A REAL TIME-SAVER!

$(x+y)*z$ is the same as $(x*z)+(y*z)$

(GENETICALLY MODIFIED FOOD **OR** GENETICALLY ENGINEERED FOOD) **AND** SAFETY

is the same as

GENETICALLY MODIFIED FOOD **AND** SAFETY **OR** GENETICALLY ENGINEERED FOOD **AND** SAFETY

IT WORKS KIND OF LIKE THE DISTRIBUTIVE PROPERTY IN ALGEBRA. I KNOW, I KNOW... BUT BEAR WITH ME.

JUST LIKE WITH THIS EQUATION, YOU CAN COMBINE THE ITEMS INSIDE THE PARENTHESES WITH WHAT'S OUTSIDE. PARENTHESES HELP SAVE TIME. INSTEAD OF DOING TWO EQUATIONS OR TWO SEARCHES, YOU JUST DO ONE.

IF YOU CAN'T REMEMBER EXACTLY HOW A WORD IS SPELLED, OR IF THERE ARE MULTIPLE VARIATIONS OF THE WORD, YOU CAN USE TOOLS CALLED **TRUNCATION** OR **WILDCARDS**. SPELLING IS NOT REALLY AN ISSUE WITH GOOGLE UNLESS YOU'RE **WAY** OFF, BUT LIBRARY SEARCHES TEND TO BE PICKY.

TRUNCATION EXPANDS OUR SEARCH WHEN WE WANT TO INCLUDE MULTIPLE DERIVATIVES OF A WORD. YOU CAN'T JUST CUT OFF PART OF THE WORD, THOUGH, OR LIBRARY SEARCHES WON'T UNDERSTAND.

SO WHEN WE SHORTEN THE TERM, WE ADD A SPECIAL CHARACTER TO LET THE SYSTEM KNOW WHAT WE'RE DOING. BY INSERTING THAT CHARACTER AT A CUT-OFF POINT, WE'RE TELLING THE SYSTEM TO FIND ALL WORDS BEGINNING WITH THAT PARTICULAR SET OF LETTERS.*

theorist theorem theories theoretical theory theorbo theorize

theor*

*EACH SYSTEM DEFINES ITS OWN "TRIGGER" CHARACTERS, SO THE SYMBOLS MAY DIFFER BETWEEN SYSTEMS. THE ASTERISK IS PRETTY COMMON.

THIS STRINGED INSTRUMENT IS CALLED A THEORBO. OBVIOUSLY NOT WHAT WE'RE LOOKING FOR, SO TRUNCATION ISN'T PERFECT. BUT MOST OF THE RESULTS **WERE** RELATED TO "THEORY," WHICH IS WHAT WE WANTED. PLUS, BY ADDING ANOTHER SEARCH TERM TO THE MIX, WE COULD PROVIDE THE SEARCH WITH EXTRA CONTEXT AND HELP NARROW OUR RESULTS APPROPRIATELY.

BE CAREFUL NOT TO CUT TOO MUCH WHEN YOU TRUNCATE! OTHERWISE, THE SEARCH CAN BE TOO GENERAL AND THE SYSTEM WILL FIND WAY TOO MANY RESULTS.*

th*

*SOME SYSTEMS REQUIRE A WORD TO HAVE A MINIMUM NUMBER OF LETTERS BEFORE YOU'RE ALLOWED TO TRUNCATE.

WILDCARDS ENABLE YOU TO "FILL IN THE BLANK" IN THE **MIDDLE** OF A WORD.

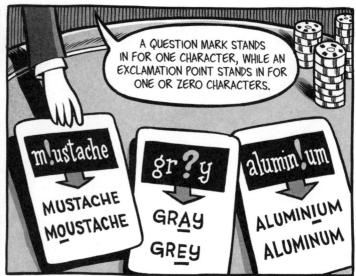

A QUESTION MARK STANDS IN FOR ONE CHARACTER, WHILE AN EXCLAMATION POINT STANDS IN FOR ONE OR ZERO CHARACTERS.

m!ustache
→
MUSTACHE
MOUSTACHE

gr?y
→
GRAY
GREY

alumin!um
→
ALUMINIUM
ALUMINUM

WILDCARDS CAN COME IN REALLY HANDY, BUT REMEMBER, EACH SYSTEM HAS ITS OWN SET OF WILDCARDS, SO CLICK ON THE "HELP" BUTTON WHEN SEARCHING BEFORE YOU USE THEM. YOU CAN USUALLY FIND THE WILDCARDS LISTED SOMEWHERE ON THE HELP PAGE. IF YOU CAN'T FIND THEM, ASK A LIBRARIAN!

fist fest flit fast foot felt fort font flat frat

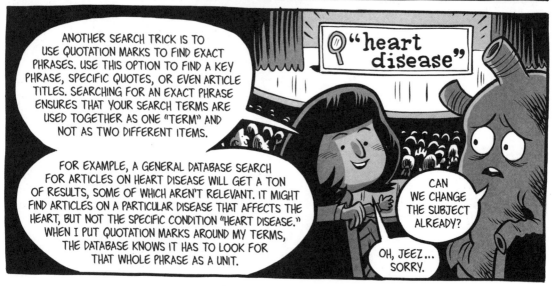

ANOTHER SEARCH TRICK IS TO USE QUOTATION MARKS TO FIND EXACT PHRASES. USE THIS OPTION TO FIND A KEY PHRASE, SPECIFIC QUOTES, OR EVEN ARTICLE TITLES. SEARCHING FOR AN EXACT PHRASE ENSURES THAT YOUR SEARCH TERMS ARE USED TOGETHER AS ONE "TERM" AND NOT AS TWO DIFFERENT ITEMS.

FOR EXAMPLE, A GENERAL DATABASE SEARCH FOR ARTICLES ON HEART DISEASE WILL GET A TON OF RESULTS, SOME OF WHICH AREN'T RELEVANT. IT MIGHT FIND ARTICLES ON A PARTICULAR DISEASE THAT AFFECTS THE HEART, BUT NOT THE SPECIFIC CONDITION "HEART DISEASE." WHEN I PUT QUOTATION MARKS AROUND MY TERMS, THE DATABASE KNOWS IT HAS TO LOOK FOR THAT WHOLE PHRASE AS A UNIT.

"heart disease"

CAN WE CHANGE THE SUBJECT ALREADY?

OH, JEEZ... SORRY.

SORRY, FELLAS... BOOKS ONLY TONIGHT.

AW, MAN!

WITHIN A LIBRARY SEARCH, YOU CAN ALSO LIMIT YOUR RESULTS ACCORDING TO CERTAIN CRITERIA, LIKE THE FORMAT (BOOK, ARTICLE, MEDIA, MAP, MUSICAL SCORE, ETC.), DATE OF PUBLICATION, FULL-TEXT OPTIONS, PEER-REVIEWED OPTIONS, AND SO ON.

FACETED SEARCHING IS SIMILAR TO THIS LIMITING PROCESS. IT'S A LITTLE LIKE SHOPPING ONLINE, CLICKING ON A "SHOP BY DEPARTMENT" LINK, THEN DROPPING DOWN LEVEL BY LEVEL UNTIL YOU FIND WHAT YOU WANT.

LIMITING BY PUBLICATION DATE IS USEFUL WHEN YOU WANT ONLY THE LATEST MATERIAL ON YOUR TOPIC, WHICH IS ESPECIALLY IMPORTANT IN SCIENTIFIC AND TECHNOLOGICAL FIELDS. WHEN THE OPTION IS AVAILABLE, YOU CAN LIMIT A SEARCH TO THE PAST FIVE OR TEN YEARS.*

ENOUGH OF THIS NONSENSE! YOU MUST BALANCE THE HUMORS!

NOT EXACTLY CUTTING-EDGE THERE, BUDDY.

*THIS IS ALSO USEFUL IF YOU'RE SEARCHING FOR HISTORICAL SOURCES, OR ITEMS PUBLISHED BEFORE A CERTAIN DATE.

LIMITING BY FORMAT HAS PRACTICAL USES, TOO. IF YOU KNOW YOU WON'T BE ABLE TO MAKE IT TO THE LIBRARY TO PICK UP A BOOK, YOU CAN LIMIT YOUR SEARCH TO E-BOOKS!

THE HUMORS, I SAY!

DUDE, ENOUGH.

CRITICAL THINKING EXERCISES

1. Write your research question or thesis statement down, and then circle the most important words or phrases. (See page 41 for an example of this.) Then come up with some synonyms or related terms for each of your original words. Use Boolean operators (AND, OR, NOT), parentheses, and/or truncation to create some search strings you could use in a library search. Try out a few different search strings, and pay attention to which results look most useful, relevant, and appropriate. What were your findings?

2. Using Google, try some of the same search strings you used for your library search. How do the results compare? How appropriate and relevant are the results from Google compared to those from the library?

3. Find two or three useful resources and look at their records. Make a list of the different subject headings assigned to each one and circle the ones that are potentially useful. Then try clicking on a few of those subject headings in the item records. What do you think about the results that you get?

4. Find the "advanced search" options in your library's search system. What is available? Which ones will likely be most useful for your topic or question?

5. Do a search for your topic. (Use one of the search strings you wrote down earlier!) Once you have a set of results, look for limiters or filters available on your results page. (These are often in a column on the left or right side of the page.) What options are available? Which ones look like they'll be most useful for you? Try adding some to your search (usually just by clicking on them). What happened? Did they make your results better or worse?

CHAPTER FOUR
JOURNALS AND DATABASES

WE'VE TALKED ABOUT LIBRARY SEARCHES, SO LET'S TALK ABOUT THAT OTHER LIBRARY RESOURCE I KEEP MENTIONING: **DATABASES**.

WHEN WE USE THE TERM "DATABASE" IN A LIBRARY, WE'RE TALKING ABOUT A SYSTEM USED SPECIFICALLY TO ACCESS DIGITAL RESOURCES LIKE E-BOOKS, ENCYCLOPEDIA ARTICLES, IMAGES, COMPANY INFORMATION, AND ESPECIALLY ACADEMIC JOURNALS AND OTHER PERIODICALS.

AND **THAT** BRINGS US TO A VERY IMPORTANT QUESTION...

...WHAT ARE PERIODICALS AND JOURNALS?

A PERIODICAL IS SOMETHING THAT COMES OUT... **PERIODICALLY**. THAT EXPLAINS IT, HUH? PERIODICALS ARE ITEMS PUBLISHED EVERY DAY OR WEEK OR MONTH OR QUARTER OR YEAR AND SO ON. THEY CAN BE MAGAZINES, NEWS-PAPERS, OR ACADEMIC JOURNALS, WHETHER THEY ARE PUBLISHED ONLINE, IN PRINT, OR BOTH. UNLIKE BOOKS, WHICH ARE PUBLISHED ONCE AND HAVE FIXED CONTENTS, PERIODICALS ARE AN ONGOING PROCESS OF GENERATING NEW CONTENT AND CONTINUAL PUBLICATION.

THOSE ARE IMAGINARY MAGAZINES, FOLKS.

POPULAR

TRADE

SCHOLARLY

PERIODICALS USUALLY FALL INTO ONE OF THREE CATEGORIES: POPULAR, TRADE/PROFESSIONAL, OR SCHOLARLY/ACADEMIC/PEER-REVIEWED. EACH CATEGORY HAS DISTINCTIVE CHARACTERISTICS YOU SHOULD REMEMBER WHEN PERFORMING ACADEMIC RESEARCH.

POPULAR RESOURCES ARE INTENDED FOR A BROAD AUDIENCE AND USUALLY DO NOT REQUIRE SPECIAL BACKGROUND KNOWLEDGE TO READ AND UNDERSTAND.

WITH POPULAR RESOURCES, YOU'LL LIKELY SEE EYE-CATCHING IMAGES AND VIDEOS, ARRESTING HEADLINES, AND PROBABLY SOME ADS. JUST KIDDING, YOU'LL **ABSOLUTELY** SEE ADS, BECAUSE WE CANNOT ESCAPE **THE AD.**

POPULAR PUBLICATIONS ARE PUBLISHED FREQUENTLY: MONTHLY, WEEKLY, EVEN DAILY. ONLINE PUBLICATIONS ARE UPDATED MULTIPLE TIMES DAILY. SEE, **CURRENCY** IS ONE OF THE MOST IMPORTANT FACTORS IN THE CONTENT OF POPULAR PUBLICATIONS, OFTEN AT THE EXPENSE OF ACCURACY. CURRENT ISSUES AND OPINION, NOT IN-DEPTH RESEARCH AND ANALYSIS, TEND TO MAKE UP THE BULK OF THESE PUBLICATIONS.

NEWS ARTICLES ARE WRITTEN FOR BROAD APPEAL, BUT ALSO TO PROVIDE TIMELY AND USEFUL INFORMATION. IN FACT, THE PRESS CAN AND SHOULD BE A VITAL PART OF A FUNCTIONING DEMOCRACY, WORKING TO ENSURE THAT PEOPLE ARE INFORMED AND THAT THOSE IN POWER ARE HELD ACCOUNTABLE.

POPULAR ARTICLES DON'T USUALLY CONTAIN FORMAL CITATIONS, BUT THEY OFTEN REFER TO SOURCES AND MAKE CLAIMS BASED ON INTERVIEWS AND INVESTIGATIONS.

☐ COMPREHENSIVE?
☐ IMPARTIAL?
☑ VERIFIABLE?

YOU SHOULD ALWAYS SEARCH FOR MORE CON-TEXT AND CONFIRMATION WHEN READING A POPULAR ARTICLE* AND REMEMBER THAT WHILE THE ARTICLE MAY BE WELL RESEARCHED, THAT DOESN'T ACTUALLY MAKE IT A RESEARCH ARTICLE.

*REMEMBER THAT A **GOOD** NEWS ORGANIZATION WILL HAVE A PATH OF EVIDENCE YOU CAN FOLLOW.

CHAPTER FOUR

PROFESSIONAL OR TRADE PUBLICATIONS SPECIALIZE IN INFORMATION RELEVANT TO A PROFESSION OR INDUSTRY AND ARE OFTEN PUBLISHED BY A PROFESSIONAL ORGANIZATION. THEY FOCUS ON TRENDS AND NEWS IN THAT FIELD, GEARED TOWARD AN AUDIENCE FAMILIAR WITH THE PROFESSION'S UNIQUE TECHNICAL JARGON. THE WRITERS AND EDITORS ASSUME THAT READERS HAVE SOME LEVEL OF PROFESSIONAL KNOWL-EDGE. YOU MIGHT EVEN FIND SOME GREAT PROFESSIONAL INFORMATION ON A BLOG OR OTHER WEBSITE.

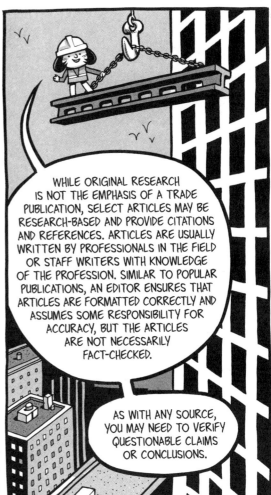

WHILE ORIGINAL RESEARCH IS NOT THE EMPHASIS OF A TRADE PUBLICATION, SELECT ARTICLES MAY BE RESEARCH-BASED AND PROVIDE CITATIONS AND REFERENCES. ARTICLES ARE USUALLY WRITTEN BY PROFESSIONALS IN THE FIELD OR STAFF WRITERS WITH KNOWLEDGE OF THE PROFESSION. SIMILAR TO POPULAR PUBLICATIONS, AN EDITOR ENSURES THAT ARTICLES ARE FORMATTED CORRECTLY AND ASSUMES SOME RESPONSIBILITY FOR ACCURACY, BUT THE ARTICLES ARE NOT NECESSARILY FACT-CHECKED.

AS WITH ANY SOURCE, YOU MAY NEED TO VERIFY QUESTIONABLE CLAIMS OR CONCLUSIONS.

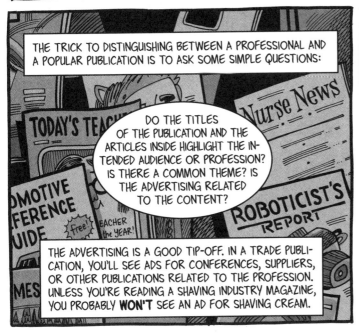

THE TRICK TO DISTINGUISHING BETWEEN A PROFESSIONAL AND A POPULAR PUBLICATION IS TO ASK SOME SIMPLE QUESTIONS:

DO THE TITLES OF THE PUBLICATION AND THE ARTICLES INSIDE HIGHLIGHT THE IN-TENDED AUDIENCE OR PROFESSION? IS THERE A COMMON THEME? IS THE ADVERTISING RELATED TO THE CONTENT?

THE ADVERTISING IS A GOOD TIP-OFF. IN A TRADE PUBLI-CATION, YOU'LL SEE ADS FOR CONFERENCES, SUPPLIERS, OR OTHER PUBLICATIONS RELATED TO THE PROFESSION. UNLESS YOU'RE READING A SHAVING INDUSTRY MAGAZINE, YOU PROBABLY **WON'T** SEE AN AD FOR SHAVING CREAM.

TRADE PUBLICATIONS ARE USUALLY RELEASED IN PRINT FORM ON A MONTHLY OR BIMONTHLY BASIS, BUT LIKE POPULAR MAGAZINES, THEIR ONLINE VERSIONS MAY BE UPDATED MORE FREQUENTLY.

OK, NOW HOW EXACTLY DOES THIS RIVET GUN WORK...?

RESEARCH

AND NOW, THE BIG ONE.

THE GOOD STUFF. THE **RESEARCH** GOLD MINE...

CURRENT Anthropology

the CHINA journal

RENAISSANCE QUARTERLY

PULMONARY CIRCULATION

t a n
THE AMERICAN NATURALIST

ACADEMIC JOURNALS. SCHOLARLY JOURNALS. PEER-REVIEWED JOURNALS. RESEARCH JOURNALS. ALL THESE NAMES REFER TO THE SAME THING: PUBLICATIONS WRITTEN BY PROFESSIONAL ACADEMICS AND RESEARCHERS, PUBLISHED BY PROFESSIONAL ORGANIZATIONS, COMMERCIAL PUBLISHERS, OR ACADEMIC INSTITUTIONS, AND FEATURING ORIGINAL RESEARCH AND ANALYSIS OF TOPICS IMPORTANT TO A PROFESSION OR ACADEMIC AREA. THE ACADEMIC JOURNAL ARTICLE IS ONE OF THE PRIMARY WAYS THAT SCHOLARS **COMMUNICATE** THEIR RESEARCH.

NOT ONLY DO ACADEMIC JOURNAL ARTICLES ALLOW SCHOLARS TO SHARE THEIR RESEARCH, THEY ALSO PROVIDE THE BASIS FOR THE RESEARCH OF OTHER SCHOLARS. RESEARCH IS A NEVER-ENDING PROCESS. RESEARCHERS UTILIZE AND ACKNOWLEDGE THE WORK OF OTHERS IN THEIR OWN ENDEAVORS. IN THIS WAY, THE BODY OF RESEARCH CONTINUES TO GROW AND ADJUST AS NEW DISCOVERIES OR APPROACHES ARE FOUND. IMAGINE EACH RESEARCH ARTICLE AS A BRICK IN A BUILDING: IT'S SUPPORTED BY THOSE LAID BEFORE IT AND SUPPORTS THOSE COMING AFTER AND BUILDING ON TOP OF IT.

RESEARCH

JOSAT
JOURNAL of OVERLY SPECIFIC ARTICLE TITLES

NATURALLY, ACADEMIC JOURNALS ARE AIMED AT A VERY PARTICULAR AUDIENCE CONSISTING OF PROFESSIONAL ACADEMICS AND RESEARCHERS, AND THEY EMPLOY TECHNICAL OR DISCIPLINE-SPECIFIC JARGON. THE TITLE OF A JOURNAL USUALLY DESCRIBES ITS FOCUS AND OFTEN INCLUDES THE WORD "JOURNAL." ARTICLE TITLES MAY BE **INTENSELY** SPECIFIC, JARGON-HEAVY, AND LONG. ARTICLES THEMSELVES TEND TO BE LONG, TOO, AND MAY FEATURE CHARTS, GRAPHS, TABLES, AND OTHER SUPPORTING ILLUSTRATIONS. YOU WON'T FIND ANY FLUFF OR MEANINGLESS IMAGES IN A JOURNAL ARTICLE.

YOU WON'T FIND ANY SHAVING CREAM ADS HERE, EITHER. **IF** THERE ARE ADS, THEY'RE FOCUSED ON SOMETHING SPECIFIC TO THE JOURNAL'S DISCIPLINE. YOU MAY SEE NOTICES FOR CONFERENCES OR OTHER PUBLICATIONS, MAYBE EVEN SPECIALIZED EQUIPMENT, TOOLS, OR RESOURCES USEFUL TO THE PROFESSION.

ACADEMIC JOURNALS ARE TYPICALLY STRAIGHT-FORWARD, LACKING EMBELLISHMENT OR BRIGHT COLORS. YOU WON'T SEE A JOURNAL COVER FEATURING THE "WORLD'S HOTTEST VOLCANOLOGIST." WELL, ALL RIGHT, YOU **MIGHT** SEE THAT COVER, BUT "HOT" WON'T MEAN WHAT YOU'RE THINKING.

WHILE THERE ARE MANY, MANY, MANY ACADEMIC JOURNALS OUT THERE, YOU'LL PROBABLY SEE THEM ONLY IN YOUR LIBRARY OR A LIBRARY DATABASE. THEY CAN BE VERY EXPENSIVE* AND HAVE A LIMITED READERSHIP, SO YOU WON'T FIND THEM ON THE NEWSSTAND NEXT TO *US WEEKLY*.

...AND THE LATEST ISSUE OF THE JOURNAL OF CLINICAL ENDOCRINOLOGY AND METABOLISM? TRY NOT TO HAVE **TOO** MUCH FUN THIS WEEKEND.

*LIBRARIES SPEND A LOT OF MONEY ON JOURNALS. USE THEM! THAT'S WHAT THEY'RE THERE FOR!

AS SUBSCRIPTION JOURNALS HAVE BECOME PRICIER (THINK HUNDREDS OR EVEN THOUSANDS OF $ PER YEAR), "OPEN ACCESS" (OR OA) JOURNALS HAVE EMERGED TO PROVIDE A FREE ALTERNATIVE (OR AT LEAST FREE TO THE READER—READ AHEAD FOR MORE INFO).

MANY OA JOURNALS WILL SHOW UP IN A DATABASE OR LIBRARY SEARCH, BUT YOU CAN ALSO USE TOOLS LIKE THE DIRECTORY OF OPEN ACCESS JOURNALS, UNPAYWALL, AND THE OPEN ACCESS BUTTON TO EASILY FIND OA CONTENT IN YOUR AREA OF INTEREST.

OPEN-ACCESS Club

• NO COVER CHARGE
• FREE PEER-REVIEW
• RESEARCH *tonite!*

VOLUME

ACADEMIC JOURNALS, DEPENDING ON THE TITLE AND DISCIPLINE, ARE PUBLISHED MONTHLY, BIMONTHLY, QUARTERLY, ANNUALLY, OR EVEN ONLY ONCE EVERY FEW YEARS.

JOURNALS OFTEN HAVE A DESIGNATED **VOLUME** AND **ISSUE** NUMBER, BUT THAT'S A REMNANT OF THE PRINT AGE, SO MANY DIGITAL-ONLY JOURNALS DON'T BOTHER. THE VOLUME NUMBER TYPICALLY REFERS TO THE WHOLE SET OF ISSUES PUBLISHED WITHIN A GIVEN TIME, USUALLY A YEAR, AND THE ISSUE NUMBER REFERS TO EACH INDIVIDUAL RELEASE.

NOT EVERY ISSUE WITHIN A VOLUME NUMBERS ITS PAGES STARTING FROM "1." JUST IMAGINE THE VOLUME IS ONE BIG COLLECTION BROKEN INTO SMALLER PARTS: THE PAGE NUMBERS IN ISSUE #1 START WITH "1," BUT ISSUES AFTER THAT MIGHT PICK UP WHERE THE PREVIOUS ISSUE LEFT OFF.

WHEN A NEW VOLUME STARTS, THE PAGE NUMBERS START OVER. AGAIN, EVEN THOUGH MOST JOURNALS ARE NOW PUBLISHED DIGITALLY, WE STILL SEE THESE ARTIFACTS FROM WHEN THEY WERE PRINT-ONLY. EACH VOLUME COULD BE BOUND TOGETHER AS A COLLECTION ON THE SHELF.

THE AUTHORS OF JOURNAL ARTICLES ARE PROFESSIONAL SCHOLARS AND RESEARCHERS WHO WRITE TO SHARE THEIR RESEARCH OR ANALYSIS, OR TO COMMENT ON OR **REVIEW** THE RESEARCH OF OTHERS. THESE AUTHORS CITE THEIR RESEARCH AND PROVIDE COMPLETE REFERENCES SO OTHERS CAN VERIFY OR ATTEMPT TO DUPLICATE THEIR RESULTS.

UNLIKE ARTICLES IN POPULAR AND TRADE PUBLICATIONS, MOST ACADEMIC JOURNAL ARTICLES GO THROUGH A PROCESS CALLED **PEER REVIEW**. THIS PROCESS HELPS ENSURE ACCURACY AND MAKES ACADEMIC ARTICLES IDEAL SOURCES FOR YOUR OWN RESEARCH.

I SHOULD CHECK THOSE REFERENCES AGAIN, I THINK...

WHEN AN ARTICLE IS PEER-REVIEWED, THE AUTHOR OF A PAPER SENDS IT TO THE EDITOR OF A JOURNAL. THAT EDITOR SENDS IT OUT TO OTHER EXPERTS WHO ARE QUALIFIED TO READ, EVALUATE, AND OFFER SUGGESTED CHANGES TO THE ARTICLE.

EDITORS SEEK OTHER VIEWPOINTS SO THAT THEY CAN DETERMINE WHETHER THERE IS A CONSENSUS OF OPINIONS ON THE PAPER. THE PROCESS ISN'T PERFECT AND MISTAKES SLIP BY EVERY ONCE IN A WHILE, WHICH IS WHY IT IS IMPORTANT FOR RESEARCHERS TO TRY TO **REPLICATE** A STUDY, TO MAKE SURE THAT RESULTS ARE ACCURATE AND STAND UP TO SCRUTINY.

RESEARCHERS ARE OFTEN PRESSURED TO COME UP WITH SOMETHING NEW AND ORIGINAL AND ARE DISCOURAGED FROM REPEATING AN EXISTING STUDY, BUT REPLICABILITY IS VITAL!

ACADEMIC WORLD SEARCH PLUS

Q _____   SELECT A FIELD ▼

AND ▼ _____

AND ▼ _____

SEARCH MODE
◉ Boolean
○ Find all search terms

TX – ALL TEXT
AU – AUTHOR
TI – TITLE
SU – SUBJECT
AB – ABSTRACT
PE – PEOPLE
PS – REVIEWS
IS – ISSN
IB – ISBN

WHEN SEARCHING A DATABASE, YOU CAN USE KEYWORDS OR DO AN ADVANCED SEARCH FOR TITLE, AUTHOR, OR SUBJECT, AMONG OTHER OPTIONS. YOU CAN ALSO USE BOOLEAN OPERATORS (**AND, OR, NOT**) BY INSERTING THEM INTO YOUR SEARCH OR BY USING THE DROP-DOWN OPTIONS.

*EXCEPT FOR A FEW REMINDERS, BECAUSE YOU'RE AWESOME AND WE WANT YOU TO SUCCEED.

WHEN YOU PERFORM A SEARCH, YOU'LL GET A LIST OF RESULTS. YOU'LL PROBABLY SEE THE ARTICLE TITLE ALONG WITH THE JOURNAL TITLE, VOLUME, ISSUE, AND PAGE NUMBERS, AND MAYBE A LINK TO THE FULL TEXT OF THE ARTICLE.

ACADEMIC WORLD SEARCH PLUS

Q comic books   SUBJECT TERMS ▼

• "Article Title" *Click Here for Full Text*
Author Last Name, First Name. *Journal Title* volume #, issue # (Date): page range.
Subjects: **Comic books**, strips, etc.; Motion pictures and **comic books**

• "Article Title" *Click Here for Full Text*
Author Last Name, First Name. *Journal Title* volume #, issue # (Date): page range.
Subjects: **Comic books**, strips, etc.; Horror **comic books**, strips, etc.

THE FULL-TEXT LIMITER IGNORES SEARCH RESULTS THAT DON'T PROVIDE ACCESS TO THE WHOLE ARTICLE.

AH, **THAT'S** WHAT I'M LOOKING FOR!

ARTICLES:

REMEMBER WHAT I SAID EARLIER ABOUT SOME JOURNALS HAVING LIMITED AVAILABILITY? ELECTRONIC JOURNALS OFTEN HAVE A "WINDOW" OF ACCESS.

ARTICLES:

SNAP!!

OW!

SOMETIMES THIS WINDOW DEPENDS ON HOW FAR BACK THE JOURNAL HAS BEEN DIGITIZED OR TRANSCRIBED:

IF JOURNAL ISSUES FROM 1965 HAVE NOT BEEN ADDED TO THE DATABASE YET, THEN YOUR WINDOW OF ACCESS WILL SHRINK.

YOU MAY NOT HAVE ACCESS TO THE LATEST ISSUES OF A JOURNAL, EITHER. THIS IS CALLED AN "EMBARGO PERIOD." SOME PUBLISHERS RESTRICT ACCESS TO THE MOST CURRENT ONLINE ARTICLES, AND SOME LIBRARIES DON'T OR CAN'T PAY FOR THE MOST RECENT MATERIAL. ASK YOUR LIBRARIAN HOW YOU CAN GET THE ARTICLE YOU NEED.

CAN I CHECK THIS JOURNAL OUT?

LIBRARY CIRCULATION DESK

I'LL NEED A CREDIT CARD, TWO LETTERS OF RECOMMENDATION, AND A DNA SAMPLE.

SORRY. THAT'S ANOTHER SLIGHT EXAGGERATION.

LIMITING A SEARCH TO FULL TEXT CAN BE TRICKY.

SMASH!

SMASH!

SMASH

SURE, YOU'LL BE ABLE TO IMMEDIATELY ACCESS AND READ THE ARTICLES, BUT YOU'LL HAVE ELIMINATED A LOT OF ARTICLES THAT MAY BE RELEVANT AND VERY RECENT, BUT NOT IMMEDIATELY ACCESSIBLE.*

I RECOMMEND USING THE FULL-TEXT OPTION ONLY WHEN YOU HAVE TO, BECAUSE THERE IS ALMOST **ALWAYS** A WAY TO TRACK DOWN AN ARTICLE. YOU MIGHT BE ABLE TO FIND IT IN ANOTHER DATABASE OR AS A HARD COPY IN YOUR LIBRARY, SO DON'T GIVE UP! YOU CAN ALSO REQUEST THE ARTICLE FROM ANOTHER LIBRARY VIA **INTERLIBRARY LOAN**.

OTHER DATABASES

HARD COPY

I.L.L.

*IN A BIT, WE'LL TALK ABOUT **ABSTRACTS**, EXPLAINING HOW EVEN PARTIAL-TEXT RESULTS CAN BE REALLY USEFUL.

RESULTS:

Title: "Concussions and High School Soccer Players: Prevention and Treatment"
Authors: Jennifer Casner and Seth Bowen
Source: *Midwest Journal of Concussion Studies*
Subject terms:
  Brain—Concussion
  Brain—Wounds & injuries
  High school athletes
  SPORTS medicine
Abstract: Many believe that soccer players do not experience significant rates of brain concussions. Research indicates, however, that high school soccer players experience concussion rates similar to or exceeding that of adolescent athletes in other full-contact sports.

articles on HIGH SCHOOL ATHLETES

articles on BRAIN CONCUSSIONS

BACK TO THE RESULTS LIST. IF YOU CLICK ON THE ARTICLE TITLE, YOU'LL GO INTO THE **RECORD**, WHERE YOU'LL GET MORE INFORMATION ON THE ARTICLE, BUT STILL NOT THE FULL TEXT. YOU'LL PROBABLY SEE THE AUTHOR(S), THE NAME OF THE PUBLICATION, THE VOLUME, ISSUE, AND PAGE NUMBERS, AND SOME SUBJECT HEADINGS.

REMEMBER THAT SUBJECT HEADINGS CAN BE A GOLD MINE. IF YOU NOTICE THAT SOME OF THEM ALIGN WELL WITH YOUR TOPIC, JOT THEM DOWN AND SAVE THEM FOR LATER...OR JUST CLICK THE LINKS AND LET THE DATABASE PROVIDE YOU WITH A LIST OF ARTICLES ON THAT SUBJECT.

AND REMEMBER, IF YOU TAKE THAT OPTION AND GET ANOTHER LIST, YOU CAN ALWAYS GO THROUGH THE LIMITING PROCESS AGAIN AND SEARCH WITHIN THAT NARROWER SET OF RESULTS.

AN ESPECIALLY USEFUL ASPECT OF A DATABASE RECORD IS THE **ABSTRACT**. THE ABSTRACT, WHICH IS NOT ALWAYS INCLUDED, PROVIDES A BRIEF SUMMARY OF THE ARTICLE. THE ARTICLE ITSELF MAY BE THIRTY PAGES LONG, BUT THE ABSTRACT EXPLAINS WHAT THE ARTICLE IS ABOUT, WHAT RESEARCH METHODS THE AUTHORS USED, AND WHAT THEIR FINDINGS WERE.

IT'S **NOT** A SUBSTITUTE FOR READING THE ENTIRE ARTICLE, BUT IT **CAN** SAVE YOU TIME. AN ABSTRACT GIVES AN IMMEDIATE SENSE OF WHETHER OR NOT AN ARTICLE WILL BE USEFUL TO YOUR RESEARCH. IF IT SEEMS RELEVANT, READ THE WHOLE ARTICLE; IF IT DOESN'T, YOU JUST SAVED YOURSELF A CHUNK OF TIME.

I HAVE TO READ ALL OF THAT?

NO. IT HAS NOTHING TO DO WITH CONCUSSIONS.

OH! THANKS.

ABSTRACT

IF YOU DECIDE THE ARTICLE IS RIGHT FOR YOU, YOU CAN OFTEN CLICK ON A LINK THAT SAYS SOMETHING LIKE "FULL TEXT" OR "PDF." THE FULL TEXT MAY OPEN DIRECTLY FROM THE RECORD PAGE, BUT THE PDF WILL MORE LIKELY BE A SEPARATE, DOWNLOADABLE FILE. PDF FILES ARE OFTEN SCANNED DIRECTLY FROM THE PRINTED ARTICLE, SO THEY'VE GOT ALL THE IMAGES, TABLES, FIGURES, AND OTHER VISUAL AIDS FROM THE ARTICLE.

YOU MIGHT ALSO HAVE THE ABILITY TO EMAIL THE ARTICLE, PRINT IT, SAVE IT—RESEARCH ON THE GO!—OR GENERATE A CITATION FOR IT.

THAT BASICALLY EXPLAINS HOW TO PERFORM A SEARCH WITHIN A DATABASE. AGAIN, BE SURE TO USE A DATABASE RELEVANT TO YOUR TOPIC, AND USE A PRECISE, WELL-PLANNED SET OF SEARCH TERMS OR SEARCH STATEMENTS. IF YOU DO, YOU'LL FIND SOME EXCELLENT RESOURCES.

BUT WHAT IF YOUR INSTRUCTOR HAS GIVEN YOU A SPECIFIC ARTICLE TO LOCATE AND READ? THEY'VE GIVEN YOU THE CITATION, BUT THAT'S IT. NEW RESEARCHERS GET THIS KIND OF ASSIGNMENT ALL THE TIME. WHAT DO YOU DO?

ONE OPTION IS TO PERFORM A LIBRARY SEARCH FOR THE **JOURNAL** TITLE AND TRACK DOWN THE RIGHT VOLUME AND ISSUE ON THE SHELF. ANOTHER OPTION IS TO SEE IF IT CAN BE FOUND IN ONE OF THE LIBRARY'S DATABASES.

CITATION DUDE

CATCH ME IF YOU CAN!

SINCE NOT EVERY JOURNAL IS INCLUDED IN EVERY DATABASE, IT'S USEFUL TO KNOW WHERE SPECIFIC JOURNALS ARE FOUND.

TRY LOOKING IN BOTH GENERAL AND SUBJECT-SPECIFIC DATABASES FOR THE JOURNAL TITLE. MOST DATABASES HAVE LINKS FOR SEARCHING THROUGH TITLES; THEN NARROW YOUR SEARCH TO A SPECIFIC VOLUME, ISSUE, AND ARTICLE. YOU CAN ALSO TRY SEARCHING GOOGLE SCHOLAR TO FIND OUT WHICH DATABASES PROVIDE ACCESS TO A JOURNAL.

MANY LIBRARIES HAVE A TOOL ON THEIR WEBSITE FOR SEARCHING FOR A SPECIFIC JOURNAL. THESE TOOLS ARE GREAT. YOU CAN SEARCH FOR A JOURNAL TITLE AND GET A LIST OF ALL THE DATABASES CARRYING THAT JOURNAL. IF YOUR LIBRARY SUBSCRIBES TO THOSE DATABASES, YOU CAN JUST CLICK A LINK, JUMP DIRECTLY TO THE JOURNAL, AND START SEARCHING BY VOLUME, ISSUE, AND ARTICLE.

THE **JOURNAL** of **SUPERHERO SCIENCE** and **CULTURE** CAN BE FOUND IN:

OPEN-ACCESS JOURNALS DATABASE

SCIENCE JOURNALS ONLINE

ART AND CULTURE ONLINE LIBRARY

IF YOUR LIBRARY DOES HAVE A DISCOVERY SERVICE, YOU MAY SEE AN OPTION ON THE LIBRARY WEBSITE LABELED "FIND BOOKS, ARTICLES, AND MORE" OR SOMETHING SIMILAR. THIS SIMPLY ALLOWS YOU TO PLUG IN YOUR SEARCH TERMS OR ARTICLE TITLES AND SEARCH MULTIPLE DATABASES. THIS CAN BE AN EASY OPTION, BUT IT ALSO MAY PROVE TO BE OVERWHELMING SINCE YOU'RE SEARCHING THROUGH A HUGE AMOUNT OF INFORMATION.

DISCOVERY SERVICE

Search

HUMANITIES DATABASE

SCIENCE DATABASE

LIBRARY CATALOG

LIBRARY ARCHIVES

SOCIAL SCIENCES DATABASE

ARTS DATABASE

ACADEMIC JOURNALS MIGHT ALSO OFFER BLOGS, PODCASTS, AND NEWS FOR FREE ON THEIR WEBSITES OR THROUGH SOCIAL MEDIA, SO IF YOU KNOW THAT THERE ARE SPECIFIC JOURNALS RELEVANT TO YOUR RESEARCH, BE SURE TO FOLLOW THEIR UPDATES. JUST DO A GOOGLE SEARCH FOR THE JOURNAL OR SKIM THROUGH SUBJECT-SPECIFIC JOURNAL LISTS IN A DATABASE OR ON *WIKIPEDIA*.

IF YOU HAVE A CITATION YOU CAN'T LOCATE WITHIN A DATABASE, OR IF YOU FIND THAT YOUR LIBRARY DOESN'T HAVE FULL-TEXT ACCESS TO AN ARTICLE, YOU CAN REQUEST AN **INTERLIBRARY LOAN**. THIS IS THE PROCESS OF BORROWING AN ITEM FROM ANOTHER LIBRARY.

OFTEN, THESE **I.L.L.S** CAN BE INITIATED WITHIN A DATABASE. YOU MIGHT SEE A LINK THAT SAYS "I.L.L.," "FIND FULL TEXT," "BORROW FROM ANOTHER LIBRARY," OR SOMETHING ALONG THOSE LINES.

EVEN IF YOU CAN'T DO THIS THROUGH THE DATABASE, YOUR LIBRARY WILL PROBABLY HAVE A REQUEST LINK ON ITS WEBSITE. TYPICALLY, THESE ARTICLES WILL BE MADE AVAILABLE DIGITALLY, MAKING THE LOAN PROCESS VERY EASY. YOU CAN ALSO DO THIS FOR BOOKS AND OTHER MEDIA, ALTHOUGH PHYSICAL ITEMS WILL HAVE TO BE SHIPPED TO YOUR LIBRARY.

CRITICAL THINKING EXERCISES

REMEMBER TO USE YOUR ONLINE TOOL TO RECORD
YOUR RESPONSES TO THE QUESTIONS.

1. Describe the process for accessing databases at your library. Use the library website or ask a librarian for help.

2. Identify at least two databases that your library has access to and that are relevant to your research or area of study. Perform a search in each one, and describe how the results are similar and different for each one.

3. Search for your topic in a library database and examine the results to identify scholarly, popular, and trade articles. List examples of each and describe how you determined which type of article each is.

4. Using a database or Google Scholar, find a scholarly article on your topic. Identify the journal title and perform a Google search for that journal. Once you get to the journal's website, explore the various features and tools available. How might these features or tools be useful to your research?

5. Using the Directory of Open Access Journals (doaj.org), identify an open access journal that covers a discipline relevant to your research topic. Go to the journal's website and look for the submission guidelines and editorial processes. Describe these in your own words. How do these guidelines help ensure high-quality research?

6. Using a database or Google Scholar, find a scholarly article on your topic. Locate and read the abstract. Based on only the abstract, how will the information in this article contribute to your own understanding of and research on your topic? What value will it add to your knowledge of your topic?

7. If you have a citation for an article that can't be accessed through a Google search, how would you go about searching for that specific article in your library's resources? Keep in mind that your library may have hundreds of databases. Is there an easy way to hunt this down with only information on the author, title, journal, etc.?

CHAPTER FIVE
SEARCHING THE OPEN WEB

NOW I'M GOING TO FOCUS ON FINDING INFORMATION ONLINE, OUTSIDE THE LIBRARY'S RESOURCES. THERE'S A HUGE AMOUNT OF INFORMATION OUT THERE, INCLUDING RESOURCES FOR RESEARCH AS WELL AS FOR ANY OTHER PURPOSE. SO MUCH OF IT WILL NOT BE RELEVANT TO YOUR WORK, AND THE QUALITY VARIES CONSIDERABLY. WE'LL TALK ABOUT WHERE AND HOW YOU CAN FIND INFORMATION USEFUL FOR ACADEMIC RESEARCH.

FIRST OF ALL, DON'T SAY WE SEARCH THE INTERNET, BECAUSE WE DON'T.

THE INTERNET IS A HUGE STRUCTURE OF NETWORKS, A BUNCH OF COMPUTERS CONNECTED TO EACH OTHER. THE INTERNET PROVIDES LINES OF COMMUNICATION, BUT THE **WORLD WIDE WEB** PROVIDES THE MEANS TO CREATE, SHARE, SEARCH, AND ACCESS INFORMATION ON TOP OF THE INTERNET.

WE SEARCH THE WEB FOR INFORMATION, AND THAT'S WHAT I'M HERE TO TALK ABOUT.

WE ALL KNOW THE WEB IS HUGE.

IT'S A MONSTROUS BEAST THAT GROWS AT A RIDICULOUS RATE, BECAUSE WE PRODUCE INFORMATION **CONSTANTLY**. WE PUBLISH AND LINK AND SHARE AND POST AND DOWNLOAD AND UPLOAD, AND IT NEVER EVER STOPS.

SO FINDING THE INFORMATION WE NEED WITH A GENERAL SEARCH OF THE WEB USING GOOGLE, BING, DUCKDUCKGO, OR ANY SEARCH ENGINE CAN BE REALLY DIFFICULT.

AND HERE'S A JAW-DROPPER: YOU CAN'T EVEN ACCESS MOST OF THE INFORMATION FLOATING AROUND OUT THERE.

YOU'VE PROBABLY LOOKED AT THE TOP OF YOUR RESULTS LIST AND THOUGHT, "12 MILLION RESULTS? THAT'S A LOT!" BUT YOU HAVE NO IDEA. THAT'S JUST THE SURFACE.

THERE'S SOMETHING CALLED THE **DEEP WEB**, WHICH SOUNDS LIKE A SCI-FI MOVIE ABOUT GIANT OCEAN SPIDERS OR SOMETHING, BUT IS ACTUALLY VERY IMPORTANT.

TO HELP EXPLAIN WHAT THE **DEEP WEB** IS, LET'S REVIEW HOW SEARCH ENGINES LIKE GOOGLE PERFORM THEIR SEARCHES.

WHEN YOU PERFORM A SEARCH, YOU'RE NOT ACTUALLY SEARCHING THE WEB. YOU'RE SEARCHING WITHIN THE SEARCH ENGINE'S OWN DATABASE OF INFORMATION ON WEBSITES.

YEP, THAT'S RIGHT. GOOGLE, BING, AND DUCKDUCKGO SEND THESE DIGITAL WEB-CRAWLERS, OR "SPIDERS," THROUGHOUT THE WEB. THEY VISIT A TON OF WEBSITES, GATHER ALL THE INFORMATION THEY CAN, AND RETURN TO HOME BASE, WHERE THEY STORE THAT INFORMATION IN A DATABASE WE CAN SEARCH.

SO, WHEN YOU DO A GOOGLE SEARCH, YOU'RE LOOKING WITHIN GOOGLE'S OWN RESOURCES, NOT DIRECTLY AT AN OUTSIDE WEB PAGE. SINCE EACH SEARCH ENGINE HAS DIFFERENT CRAWLERS AND A DIFFERENT RANKING SYSTEM, YOU'LL GET DIFFERENT RESULTS WITH DIFFERENT TOOLS.*

YES, I SAID "DIFFERENT" FOUR TIMES IN THAT SENTENCE, BUT I WANT THAT POINT TO BE CLEAR:

NO TWO SEARCH ENGINES ARE EQUAL.

SEARCH ENGINE DATABASE

web-site

web-site

web-site

*SEE "How Search Organizes Information"
(https://www.google.com/search/howsearchworks/crawling-indexing/).

AS COOL AS SEARCH ENGINES AND SPIDERS ARE, THEY CAN'T ENTER CERTAIN TYPES OF WEBSITES. WEB DESIGNERS CAN BUILD SITES THAT KEEP CRAWLERS OUT. IF YOU HAVE TO PAY TO ACCESS A SITE, A SPIDER CAN'T GET IN, INVESTIGATE, AND SEND INFO BACK TO HOME BASE. IF YOU HAVE TO USE A PASSWORD TO ACCESS A SITE? SAME PROBLEM.

IN MOST CASES, A GENERAL WEB SEARCH WON'T DIG THROUGH LIBRARY RESOURCES, EITHER. SINCE BOOKS AND ACADEMIC PUBLICATIONS TEND TO HIDE OUT IN LIBRARY SEARCHES AND DATABASES, THIS CAN BE A BIG DEAL.

NO SPIDERS ALLOWED!!

AW, MAN!

GOOGLE, BING, AND DUCKDUCKGO SEARCHES CAN BE PARTIALLY OR COMPLETELY BLIND TO THE INFORMATION KEPT BEHIND THOSE BARRIERS. SO YOU'RE MISSING OUT ON A LOT OF INFORMATION BY USING GENERAL WEB SEARCHES INSTEAD OF DATABASE SEARCHES. THAT'S INEXCUSABLE WHEN YOU'RE RESEARCHING AN ACADEMIC PAPER.

PLUS, IF YOU'RE A COLLEGE STUDENT, YOUR INSTITUTION PAYS FOR YOUR CAMPUS TO HAVE ACCESS TO EXCELLENT DATABASES FOR YOUR WORK, SO TAKE ADVANTAGE OF THOSE RESOURCES.

SOAP

BUT BACK TO THIS DEEP WEB CONCEPT. IMAGINE YOU ARE STANDING OUTSIDE LOOKING UP AT THE NIGHT SKY.

THERE'S AN ENTIRE UNIVERSE OUT THERE, BUT YOU CAN'T SEE **ALL** OF IT. THERE'S SO **MUCH**, AND THINGS ARE **SO FAR AWAY** THAT YOU CAN'T SEE EVEN THE FAINTEST BIT OF LIGHT FROM THEM. THERE MIGHT BE AN INFINITE AMOUNT OF STUFF IN DEEP SPACE, BUT YOU CAN'T VIEW MOST OF IT WITH THE NAKED EYE.

IMAGINE THE STARS YOU CAN SEE ARE LIKE THE RESULTS OF A WEB SEARCH. THE REST? THE DEEP WEB.* THE STUFF THAT CAN'T BE ACCESSED THROUGH A GENERAL SEARCH ENGINE LIKE GOOGLE.

*NOT THE SAME THING AS THE "DARK WEB," WHICH CONSISTS OF BOTH LEGITIMATE AND ILLEGAL "WEBSITES THAT CAN ONLY BE ACCESSED THROUGH SPECIAL ROUTING SOFTWARE" LIKE TOR. FOR MORE INFORMATION, SEE Weaving the Dark Web by R. Gehl.

YOU CAN SEE FAMILIAR CONSTELLATIONS, RELIABLE AND STEADY, BUT YOU WANT **MORE**. YOU NEED TO SEE PAST THEM AND DISCOVER SOMETHING NEW.

BUT YOU'VE GOT ALL THIS JUNK BLOCKING THE VIEW, DISTRACTING YOU, AND IT'S EASY TO FORGET THAT THERE IS SO MUCH MORE OUT THERE. YOU NEED A TOOL TO HELP YOU SEE FARTHER AND DEEPER.

NOW, IMAGINE BYPASSING ALL THAT JUNK. IMAGINE HAVING THE POWER TO SEE DEEPER INTO SPACE— TO SEE ALL THE THINGS PREVIOUSLY BEYOND SIGHT—

—IN GREAT DETAIL AND CLARITY!

STARGAZER 3000

THAT'S WHAT ADDING LIBRARY AND ARTICLE DATABASE SEARCHES TO YOUR GENERAL WEB SEARCHING CAN DO. THAT'S DEEP WEB VERSUS SURFACE WEB. LIBRARY RESOURCES CAN ELIMINATE CLUTTER AND IN-CREASE THE DEPTH AND QUALITY OF YOUR SEARCHES.

LIKE DEEP SPACE, THE DEEP WEB IS A VAST PLACE, BUT SOME REALLY INTERESTING AND USEFUL THINGS OCCUR THERE. THE DEEP WEB IS **WAY** BIGGER THAN THE "SEARCH-ABLE" WEB, AND THERE **ARE** VARIOUS WAYS TO SEARCH AND NAVIGATE THE DEEP WEB OR **PARTS** OF THE DEEP WEB (LIKE A LIBRARY DATABASE).

THAT'S GETTING OUTSIDE THE SCOPE OF THIS BOOK. BUT DON'T JUST ASSUME THAT IF IT DOESN'T SHOW UP IN YOUR GOOGLE RESULTS, IT DOESN'T EXIST!

EACH SEARCH ENGINE FUNCTIONS A BIT DIFFERENTLY. STILL, THERE ARE BASIC STRATEGIES YOU CAN USE IN A GENERAL WEB SEARCH. REMEMBER, SEARCHING THE WEB WILL DIFFER FROM SEARCHING A LIBRARY DATABASE IN TERMS OF BOTH RESULTS **AND** SEARCH TECHNIQUE.

MAKE SURE YOUR GENERAL WEB SEARCH IS PRECISE AND CONTAINS MULTIPLE RELEVANT TERMS.* FORMULATE YOUR SEARCH TERMS CAREFULLY, AND DON'T WASTE TIME WITH FLUFF WORDS THAT DON'T HELP SPECIFY WHAT YOU'RE LOOKING FOR.

SEARCH TIME

high school soccer concussion prevention

*LUCKILY, YOU'VE ALREADY MASTERED THOSE SKILLS!

SEARCH ENGINES ALSO HAVE **ADVANCED SEARCHING** OPTIONS, BUT THEY'RE NOT QUITE LIKE THOSE FOUND IN LIBRARY SEARCHES.

THE ADVANCED SEARCH OPTION MIGHT BE TOUGH TO FIND. WITH GOOGLE, YOU HAVE TO EITHER SEARCH FOR "ADVANCED SEARCH" OR SEARCH FOR YOUR TERMS, **THEN** CLICK THE "SETTINGS" OPTION TO LOCATE THE "ADVANCED SEARCH" LINK.

TIME   ADVANCED SEARCH

YOU'LL SEE THE ADVANCED SEARCH LACKS SUBJECT, AUTHOR, OR TITLE SEARCH OPTIONS. YOU **WILL** BE ABLE TO LIMIT OR EXPAND YOUR SEARCH A FEW DIFFERENT WAYS, HOWEVER.

YOU CAN ESSENTIALLY REPLICATE BOOLEAN LIMITERS (**AND, OR, NOT**) BY USING ADVANCED SEARCH OPTIONS.

YOU MIGHT BE OFFERED MULTIPLE SEARCH BARS. ONE MIGHT SEARCH FOR "ALL THESE WORDS," WHICH IS SIMILAR TO AN "AND" SEARCH.

A BAR LABELED "THIS EXACT WORD OR PHRASE" FUNCTIONS AS QUOTATION MARKS, ISOLATING THAT PRECISE STRING OF WORDS WITHIN A WEBSITE.

BOOLEAN

- AND
- OR
- NOT

GOOGLE ADVANCED

- ALL THESE WORDS
- ANY of THESE WORDS
- NONE OF THESE WORDS

GOOGLE SHORTCUT

- JUST TYPE IN YOUR TERMS— GOOGLE AUTOMATICALLY TREATS IT AS AN **AND** SEARCH
- TYPE IN **OR** BETWEEN YOUR TERMS
- PUT A **MINUS** SIGN NEXT TO WORDS YOU DON'T WANT

IN MANY WAYS, THIS IS EASIER THAN A LIBRARY SEARCH. IT'S MORE OBVIOUS EXACTLY HOW TERMS ARE USED TO NARROW OR EXPAND SEARCHES. JUST PLUG YOUR SEARCH TERMS INTO THE APPROPRIATE BOXES AND GO!

AN ADVANCED SEARCH ALSO LETS YOU LIMIT A SEARCH TO A PARTICULAR PART OF A WEB PAGE, LIKE THE TITLE OR MAIN TEXT. YOU CAN SOMETIMES LIMIT BY LANGUAGE, LAST UPDATE, FILE TYPE, AND THE DOMAIN TYPE (.COM, .EDU, .GOV, .ORG, ETC.).

MINUS SIGN

USE TO ELIMINATE A SEARCH TERM

EXAMPLE

Q lincoln -car

SITE: SITE WITH COLON

USE TO SEARCH WITHIN A SPECIFIC WEBSITE

EXAMPLE

Q site:speeches.com lincoln

YOU CAN ALSO LIMIT A SEARCH TO A SPECIFIC WEBSITE. GO DIRECTLY TO A SITE AND USE ITS INTERNAL SEARCH ENGINE (WHICH MIGHT NOT BE THAT GREAT), OR JUST PUT THAT WEBSITE'S ADDRESS INTO THE APPROPRIATE SEARCH BAR IN AN ADVANCED SEARCH.

" " QUOTATION MARKS

USE QUOTATION MARKS TO DEFINE AN EXACT PHRASE

EXAMPLE

Q "a house divided"

YOU DON'T HAVE TO USE THE ADVANCED SEARCH TO LIMIT OR BROADEN A SEARCH. YOU CAN NORMALLY USE CERTAIN SYMBOLS (OR OPERATORS) TO DESIGNATE A PARTICULAR ACTION WITHIN THE GENERAL SEARCH BAR. THESE ACTIONS ARE IDENTICAL TO WHAT YOU CAN DO WITHIN THE ADVANCED SEARCH.

FOR EXAMPLE, ADDING A MINUS SIGN ("-") BEFORE A WORD CAN ELIMINATE THAT TERM FROM YOUR SEARCH, LIKE USING "NOT." ADDING "SITE:" (WITH A COLON) BEFORE A WEBSITE NAME WILL ALLOW YOU TO USE THE SEARCH ENGINE TO SEARCH SPECIFICALLY WITHIN THAT SITE. QUOTATION MARKS ("PHRASE") WILL FIND AN EXACT PHRASE.

YOU CAN SOMETIMES USE TRADITIONAL BOOLEAN OPERATORS IN COOPERATION WITH THESE SYMBOLS. MOST SEARCH ENGINES ASSUME AN "AND" BETWEEN YOUR SEARCH TERMS, SO YOU DON'T NEED TO INCLUDE ONE IN YOUR SEARCH STATEMENT. EACH SEARCH ENGINE IS DIFFERENT, SO BE SURE TO CLICK ON A "HELP" LINK TO GET TIPS ON HOW TO STREAMLINE YOUR SEARCHING.

ALWAYS KNOW WHAT TOOLS YOU'VE GOT AROUND!

USING THESE TIPS AND STRATEGIES, YOU CAN EXERCISE A LOT OF CONTROL OVER YOUR RESULTS.

THAT BEING SAID, THE SEARCH ENGINE WILL ALSO EXERT CONTROL THROUGH THE USE OF ALGORITHMS.

DO YOU EVEN ALGORITHM, BRO?

ALGORITHMS ARE SIMPLY RULES AND PROCEDURES THAT HELP US GET FROM AN INPUT TO AN OUTPUT. SO, IN THE CASE OF A SEARCH ENGINE, HOW DOES YOUR SEARCH (THE INPUT) TURN INTO A LIST OF RESULTS (THE OUTPUT)?

WE OFTEN DON'T KNOW EXACTLY WHAT THESE ALGORITHMS LOOK LIKE SINCE THEY'RE KEPT PRETTY SECRET BY THE COMPANIES THAT DESIGN THEM, BUT WE ARE ABLE TO INFER SOME THINGS, JUST BY EXAMINING THE RESULTS.

INPUT

OUTPUT

ONE THING WE DO KNOW IS THAT SEARCH ENGINE ALGORITHMS ARE COMPUTER CODE THAT IS DESIGNED AND DEFINED BY **FALLIBLE, IMPERFECT HUMANS** (LIKE YOU AND ME), WORKING WITHIN AN ENVIRONMENT THAT MAY VALUE PROFIT OVER FAIRNESS, EQUITY, OR ACCURACY.

THEREFORE, IT IS IMPORTANT TO UNDERSTAND THAT SEARCH ENGINES LIKE GOOGLE ARE NOT NEUTRAL, AND THE CODE CAN AND WILL CARRY THE BIASES OF THE PEOPLE, ORGANIZATIONS, AND EVEN SOCIETIES THAT DESIGN THEM.

oooooohh... aaaahhh...

IN OTHER WORDS, THE INSTRUCTIONS THAT SEARCH ALGORITHMS FOLLOW WILL ALWAYS BE PROBLEMATIC AND CAN BE IMPROVED, BUT IT'S TOUGH TO DO THAT WHEN THE GENERAL PUBLIC DOESN'T EXACTLY KNOW WHAT'S GOING ON IN THE "BLACK BOX."

CHAPTER FIVE

THE *WALL STREET JOURNAL** FOUND IN 2019 THAT GOOGLE ACTUALLY CHANGES ITS SEARCH ALGORITHMS FREQUENTLY AND PAYS THOUSANDS OF PEOPLE TO EVALUATE ITS RESULT-RANKING QUALITY.

THIS MAY SOUND LIKE A GOOD THING UNTIL WE REALIZE HOW PROBLEMATIC IT IS THAT A FOR-PROFIT COMPANY IS ESSENTIALLY IN CHARGE OF HOW HUNDREDS OF MILLIONS OF PEOPLE PERCEIVE AND ACCESS INFORMATION AND THAT THEIR PROCESSES LACK TRANSPARENCY.

THIS INVESTIGATION ALSO FOUND THAT GOOGLE ADJUSTED SEARCH RESULTS TO FAVOR BIG BUSINESSES, ALL WHILE PORTRAYING THEMSELVES AS A NEUTRAL PROVIDER OF THE WORLD'S INFORMATION.

*SEE "How Google Interferes with Its Search Algorithms and Changes Your Results" by K. Grind, S. Schechner, R. McMillan, and J. West (https://www.wsj.com/articles/how-google-interferes-with-its-search-algorithms-and-changes-your-results-11573823753).

SEARCH ENGINES WILL ALWAYS BE BIASED IN SOME WAYS, BECAUSE THEY ARE BUILT TO CATEGORIZE, PRIORITIZE, AND SORT INFORMATION. THERE WILL BE VALUE JUDGMENTS BAKED INTO THE PROCESS FOR RANKING SEARCH RESULTS. SOMETIMES THIS BIAS CAN BE HARMFUL TO INDIVIDUALS OR GROUPS OF PEOPLE.

FOR EXAMPLE, DR. SAFIYA NOBLE* FOUND OVER SEVERAL YEARS THAT SEARCHING GOOGLE FOR THE TERMS "BLACK GIRLS" OR "ASIAN GIRLS" (OR OTHER PHRASES THAT SPECIFICALLY REFER TO WOMEN OF COLOR) RETURNED A LOT OF HYPERSEXUALIZED RESULTS AT THE TOP OF THE LIST, WHILE SEARCHES LIKE "BEAUTIFUL," "DOCTORS," AND "PROFESSOR STYLE" RESULTED IN IMAGES THAT DISPROPORTIONATELY FEATURED WHITE PEOPLE.

THESE ARE ONLY TWO EXAMPLES OF HOW SEARCH ENGINE RESULTS CAN REINFORCE STEREOTYPES, PRESENT INACCURATE INFORMATION, AND POTENTIALLY MISLEAD OR OPPRESS USERS.

*SEE *Algorithms of Oppression* by S. Noble.

SINCE DR. NOBLE BEGAN HER RESEARCH, GOOGLE HAS DONE A LOT TO FIX THESE PROBLEMS, AND WHILE YOU LIKELY WON'T FIND SEXUALLY EXPLICIT WEBSITES FOR THESE SEARCHES ANYMORE, GOOGLE AND MANY OTHER TECH COMPANIES OPERATE WITHIN A FRAMEWORK THAT FAVORS WHITE HETEROSEXUAL MEN. LACK OF DIVERSITY AND PROFIT-DRIVEN BUSINESS MODELS ARE MAJOR LIMITATIONS TO BIG TECH'S ABILITY TO HELP US PROCESS INFORMATION.

THESE PROBLEMS PLAY OUT IN SIGNIFICANT AND HARMFUL WAYS QUITE FREQUENTLY. ALGORITHMS, WHICH SUPPOSEDLY MAKE UNBIASED, STATISTICALLY SOUND DECISIONS FOR US, ARE APPLIED IN WAYS THAT RESULT IN **MORE** INEQUALITY.

ALGORITHMS HELP DECIDE WHETHER OR NOT PEOPLE GET LOANS AND JOB INTERVIEWS AND HOW PRISON SENTENCES, WORK SCHEDULES, AND INSURANCE RATES ARE DETERMINED.

THEY CAN ALSO PREVENT PEOPLE FROM GETTING THE PUBLIC SERVICES THEY NEED, ALL IN THE NAME OF GREATER "EFFICIENCY" AND UNDER THE GUISE OF NEUTRALITY OR UTILITY.*

*SEE Weapons of Math Destruction by C. O'Neil, Automating Inequality by V. Eubanks, Race after Technology by R. Benjamin, "The Myth of the Impartial Machine" by A. Feng and S. Wu (https://parametric.press/issue-01/the-myth-of-the-impartial-machine/), AND "The Miseducation of Dylann Roof" by H. Beirich, R. Cohen, and W. Via (https://www.splcenter.org/files/miseducation-dylann-roof).

BUT THE THING IS, THESE ALGORITHMIC PROCESSES ARE OFTEN BASED ON FLAWED, BIASED, OR INCOMPLETE DATA AND FREQUENTLY SERVE TO EXACERBATE PROBLEMS. MANY OF US TEND TO SAY, "OH, WELL, A MATHEMATICAL PROCESS CAN'T BE BIASED. IT'S MATH!" BUT REMEMBER THAT IT'S NOT **JUST** MATH. IT'S THE UNDERLYING DATA AND DESIGN GOALS THAT FEED THE PROCESS. AND IF WE START FROM A FLAWED PLACE, EFFORTS TO BE MORE "EFFICIENT" JUST RESULT IN FASTER AND MORE EXTREME INEQUALITY AND DISCRIMINATION.*

*IF YOU'RE INTERESTED IN LEARNING MORE AND TAKING ACTION, CHECK OUT THE WORK OF JOY BUOLAMWINI AND THE ALGORITHMIC JUSTICE LEAGUE AT www.ajlunited.org.

WE CAN SEE THAT WHEN "BIG TECH" DOESN'T TAKE UNDERLYING SOCIAL ISSUES INTO ACCOUNT, IT OFTEN MAKES THINGS WORSE. THAT'S WHY YOU SHOULD NOT ASSUME THAT THE FIRST ITEMS ON A RESULTS PAGE ARE THE BEST (MORE ON THAT LATER) AND REMEMBER THAT YOU NOW HAVE PLENTY OF TOOLS AT YOUR DISPOSAL TO TAKE MORE CONTROL OVER YOUR SEARCHES.

ALL WEBSITES ABOUT INFORMATION LITERACY

.com .mil .info .edu .net .gov .org

SEARCH ENGINES AREN'T THE ONLY GATEWAYS TO INFORMATION ON THE OPEN WEB. DEPENDING ON YOUR RESEARCH, IT MIGHT BE A GOOD IDEA TO CHECK OUT VARIOUS GOVERNMENT, PUBLIC, AND NONPROFIT ORGANIZATIONS' WEBSITES.

YOU CAN SEARCH A SPECIFIC DOMAIN, LIKE .GOV, USING A GOOGLE ADVANCED SEARCH. FOR EXAMPLE, LET'S SAY I WANTED TO FIND MATERIAL ON PUBLIC INFORMATION LITERACY POLICY AND INITIATIVES. I COULD DO A GOOGLE SEARCH FOR "INFORMATION LITERACY" AND LIMIT THE SEARCH TO .GOV SITES, AND I WOULD GET RESULTS ON THAT TOPIC FROM FEDERAL, STATE, AND SOME LOCAL GOVERNMENT SITES.

THERE'S AN OVERWHELMING VOLUME OF OFFICIAL INFORMATION PUBLISHED BY THE GOVERNMENT, AN INCREASING AMOUNT OF WHICH CAN BE FOUND ONLINE.

THE US GOVERNMENT PRINTING OFFICE (GPO) KEEPS A GREAT COLLECTION OF DIGITAL RESOURCES DETAILING THE INNER WORKINGS AND PROCESSES OF OUR GOVERNMENT AT www.gpo.gov.

THE LIBRARY OF CONGRESS PROVIDES MANY DIGITAL RESOURCES RELATED TO THE HISTORY OF THE UNITED STATES, AND IT OFFERS LINKS TO VARIOUS GOVERN-MENTAL DEPARTMENTS, OFFICES, AND FOUNDATIONS, MANY OF WHICH OFFER THEIR OWN PUBLICATIONS AND RESEARCH. FIND IT ALL AT www.loc.gov.

www.science.gov COMPILES AND LETS YOU SEARCH THROUGH VAST AMOUNTS OF SCIENTIFIC RESEARCH FROM MULTIPLE GOVERNMENT AGENCIES WITH ONE SEARCH, AND www.congress.gov SUPPLIES AN ENORMOUS AMOUNT OF LEGISLATIVE INFORMATION.

THE FEDERAL GOVERNMENT ALSO DEDICATES BILLIONS OF DOLLARS EACH YEAR TOWARD FUNDING RESEARCH.

IN GENERAL, THERE HAS BEEN PROGRESS IN MAKING FEDERALLY FUNDED RESEARCH MORE ACCESSIBLE TO THE PUBLIC, ALTHOUGH RECENTLY THERE HAVE BEEN POLITICALLY DRIVEN EFFORTS TO DEEMPHASIZE FUNDED RESEARCH AND POLICY IN AREAS SUCH AS CLIMATE CHANGE AND OTHER ENVIRONMENTAL CONCERNS.

IN ADDITION TO RESEARCH AND INFORMATION MADE AVAILABLE BY THE GOVERNMENT AND OTHER PUBLICLY ORIENTED ORGANIZATIONS, LIBRARIES, ARCHIVES, AND MUSEUMS HAVE EXHIBITIONS AND SPECIAL COLLECTIONS THAT ARE SEARCHABLE ONLINE AND INCREASINGLY AVAILABLE AS DIGITAL COLLECTIONS. FOR AN EXAMPLE, SEE THE SMITHSONIAN INSTITUTE ONLINE AT www.si.edu.

GOT ONE MORE THING TO LOAD UP FOR YA.

I DON'T THINK IT'LL FIT...

APOLLO 11 ARTIFACTS

WHAT IF YOU DON'T KNOW WHICH ORGANIZATIONS ARE DOING RESEARCH ON YOUR TOPIC? TAKE A CLOSER LOOK AT THE AUTHORS OF SOURCES YOU HAVE ALREADY FOUND TO DETERMINE WHERE THEY WORK OR WHO IS FUNDING THEIR RESEARCH.

BE FLEXIBLE AND DIRECT WITH YOUR SEARCHES, AND DON'T BE AFRAID TO PLUG IN VARIANTS OF YOUR TERMS. YOU MIGHT ALSO ADD "RESEARCH" TO YOUR SEARCH TERMS TO EMPHASIZE THAT FOCUS. YOU MIGHT FIND WHOLE TEAMS OF RESEARCHERS DEVOTED TO YOUR TOPIC!

WE'RE GONNA BEAT THE PEER REVIEW OUTTA YOU!!

DISSERTATION DEFENSE!

DATA

RUTHERFORD STATE RESEARCHERS

ALL RIGHT, FOLKS. IT'S DOWN TO THE WIRE. YOU GET OUT THERE AND DO WHAT YOU DO. RESEARCH! RESEARCH WITH EVERYTHING YOU'VE GOT!

OF COURSE, YOU WILL NEED TO EVALUATE EACH RESOURCE TO DETERMINE WHETHER OR NOT YOU CAN TRUST THE INFORMATION. WE'LL GET INTO THAT MORE LATER, BUT HERE'S A QUICK EXAMPLE:

I DID A SIMPLE GOOGLE SEARCH FOR "ASTEROID RESEARCH" AND FOUND LEGITIMATE RESEARCH DONE BY THE ASTEROID DEFLECTION RESEARCH COLLABORATION (YES, A REAL PLACE) ABOUT WAYS TO KNOCK THREATENING ASTEROIDS OFF COURSE. I ALSO FOUND A WEBSITE THAT PRESENTED AN EMOTIONAL APPEAL TO READERS ABOUT THE INEVITABILITY OF A LARGE ASTEROID STRIKING EARTH IN THE HOPE OF RAISING FUNDS FOR RESEARCH EQUIPMENT.

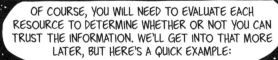

RELEVANT RESEARCH CONTENT

THAT WAS A FAIRLY VAGUE SEARCH IN THE FIRST PLACE, BUT IT SHOWS THAT YOU WILL FIND MANY SITES DEDICATED TO A TOPIC AND YOU WILL NEED TO EVALUATE THEM IN ORDER TO TARGET RELEVANT CONTENT.

CHAPTER FIVE

NO EXAMINATION OF WEB SEARCHING IS COMPLETE WITHOUT DISCUSSING WIKIPEDIA.

MANY OF YOU MAY HAVE BEEN TOLD TO NEVER USE WIKIPEDIA FOR YOUR RESEARCH, BUT YOU PROBABLY USED IT ANYWAY, RIGHT?

WELL, WIKIPEDIA CAN BE REALLY USEFUL, BUT IN ORDER TO USE IT **EFFECTIVELY**, YOU NEED TO KNOW A FEW THINGS.

RESEARCH MARAT...

MY OPINION? WIKIPEDIA IS A FANTASTIC PLACE... TO **START** YOUR RESEARCH.

YOU MAY NOT WANT TO CITE WIKIPEDIA BECAUSE IT IS NOT ORIGINAL RESEARCH—IT JUST COMPILES AND SYNTHESIZES INFORMATION TO GIVE YOU AN OVERVIEW—SO IT IS NOT CONSIDERED AN "ACADEMIC" SOURCE BY MANY STANDARDS.

NOT ACCURATE

VISITS WIKIPEDIA...

...ACHIEVES COSMIC AWARENESS.

CLICK

IT'S OK TO START WITH A WIKIPEDIA ARTICLE TO GAIN A GENERAL SENSE OF A TOPIC AND TO FIND POSSIBLE ANGLES FOR RESEARCH—YOU HAVE TO KNOW WHAT KINDS OF QUESTIONS TO ASK TO CONDUCT PROPER RESEARCH, AFTER ALL—BUT READING THE WIKIPEDIA ARTICLE ON CHEMOTHERAPY WON'T BE ENOUGH FOR YOU TO BE ABLE TO WRITE A PAPER ON THE TOPIC.

IF YOU START WITH *WIKIPEDIA*, USE THE ARTICLE(S) ONLY TO LAY THE GROUNDWORK. INTRODUCE YOURSELF TO DIFFERENT ASPECTS OF THE TOPIC. GET FAMILIAR WITH THE TERMINOLOGY ASSOCIATED WITH THE TOPIC SO YOU CAN START ASSEMBLING GOOD KEYWORDS AND SEARCH STATEMENTS FOR WHEN YOU SEARCH IN LIBRARY RESOURCES.

Bibliography

America: History and Life. Ipswich, MA: EBSCO Publishing, 1990s–.
www.ebscohost.com/academic/.
Student's Guide to History. 10th ed. Boston: Bedford/St. M
riography: Ancient, Medieval and Modern. 3rd ed. Chicag
History. 14 vols. Cambridge: Cambridge University Pres
http://histories.cambridge.org/.
Danky, Ja lip, and Maureen Hady. *African-American Newspapers and P*
Frick, Elizabeth, Hi ibliography. Cambri MA: Harvard

THE MOST HELPFUL PART OF A *WIKIPEDIA* OR AN ENCYCLOPEDIA ARTICLE IS THE BIBLIOGRAPHY, WORKS CITED, NOTES, REFERENCES, OR WHATEVER ELSE IT'S CALLED. THIS LIST OF BOOKS AND ARTICLES IS BASICALLY AN INSTANT LIST OF SOURCES YOU CAN SEEK OUT, AND YOU GOT IT WITHOUT DOING A SINGLE SEARCH. USE IT!

ONE WEAKNESS OF *WIKIPEDIA* IS ALSO WHAT MAKES IT GREAT: ANYONE CAN UPDATE IT.

SO WHILE THERE MAY BE PEOPLE ADDING BAD INFO, A LOT OF THE PEOPLE WHO USE THIS RESOURCE ACT AS "FACT-CHECKERS," DISPUTING ERRONEOUS OR MALICIOUS ADDITIONS. YOU CAN ACTUALLY TAKE A LOOK AT THE "TALK" AND "HISTORY" TABS ON A *WIKIPEDIA* PAGE AND SEE WHAT EDITS HAVE OCCURRED AND IF THERE IS ANY CONVERSATION OR DEBATE ABOUT THE CONTENTS.

THAT INFO CAN PROVIDE MORE INSIGHT INTO WHETHER YOU CAN TRUST THE CONTENT AND TO WHAT DEGREE.

STILL, *WIKIPEDIA* ISN'T AS THOROUGH OR PRECISE AS MOST "OFFICIAL" REFERENCE SOURCES. CITATIONS ARE OFTEN LACKING, FACTS MAY BE OFF, THE EDITORIAL STANDARDS CAN BE INCONSISTENT, AND CORRECTIONS MAY BE SLOW IN COMING.

IF YOU HAPPEN TO READ AN ARTICLE WHILE THERE'S STILL A GLARING MISTAKE ON A PAGE, YOU'VE GOT A PROBLEM.

BUT GUESS WHAT? **YOU** CAN UPDATE *WIKIPEDIA* TOO, SO IF YOU SEE SOMETHING THAT IS INACCURATE, YOU CAN CONTRIBUTE YOUR OWN KNOWLEDGE TO THE SYSTEM, CREATING A BETTER RESOURCE FOR EVERYONE.

SO, WHILE I DON'T WANT TO DISCOURAGE YOU FROM USING *WIKIPEDIA*—I USE IT ALL THE TIME, AND IT'S WONDERFUL— YOU SHOULD USE IT ONLY AS A STARTING POINT.

WIKIPEDIA IS A GENERAL REFERENCE RESOURCE, BUT DON'T USE IT AS YOUR MAIN SOURCE OF INFORMATION FOR ACADEMIC RESEARCH. YOU NEED SOURCES THAT STAND UP TO **EVALUATION**.

AND IF YOU WANT TO KNOW WHAT **THAT** MEANS, SEE THE NEXT CHAPTER!

CHAPTER FIVE

LIKE ALL SOURCES OF INFORMATION, *WIKI-PEDIA* IS NOT WITHOUT ITS FLAWS. MANY USERS AND EDITORS, ALONG WITH SOCIAL SCIENCE RESEARCHERS, HAVE RAISED CONCERNS ABOUT *WIKIPEDIA'S* BIAS AGAINST WOMEN AND PEOPLE OF COLOR. THERE ARE EVEN *WIKIPEDIA* PAGES ABOUT IT!*

*https://en.wikipedia.org/wiki/Gender_bias_on_Wikipedia; https://en.wikipedia.org/wiki/Racial_bias_on_Wikipedia

THE MAJORITY OF CONTRIBUTORS WHO CREATE, EDIT, AND MAINTAIN *WIKIPEDIA* ARTICLES ARE MEN, WHICH HAS LED TO LESS COVERAGE ON TOPICS ABOUT WOMEN OR THAT MAY BE OF PARTICULAR INTEREST TO WOMEN. IT ALSO MEANS THAT THE PERSPECTIVE OF WOMEN IS MISSING FROM MUCH OF THE CONTENT ON THE SITE. OVER THE PAST FEW YEARS, MORE EFFORTS HAVE BEEN MADE TO IMPROVE *WIKIPEDIA* CONTENT ABOUT AND BY WOMEN, BUT THERE IS STILL A LONG WAY TO GO.

NONE OF THIS MEANS THAT THE ARTICLES THAT ARE ON *WIKIPEDIA* ARE INHERENTLY **BAD**, BUT SIMPLY THAT THERE IS A LOT OF INFORMATION THAT'S NOT EVEN THERE FOR PEOPLE TO FIND IN THE FIRST PLACE. AS WITH GOOGLE, PART OF THE PROBLEM IS THAT THESE SITES AND TOOLS ARE SO POPULAR, MANY OF US COME TO SEE THEM AS COMPLETE AND INFALLIBLE, BUT IF WE DO THAT, THEN WE END UP INADVERTENTLY ACCEPTING THEIR FLAWS AS FACTS.

ENCOURAGE EXCELLENT EDITING

IF THESE RESOURCES THAT ARE USED MILLIONS, EVEN BILLIONS, OF TIMES DAILY PROVIDE US WITH FALSE OR INCOMPLETE INFORMATION, THAT MALICE OR OVERSIGHT CAN BECOME COMMON-PLACE AND HARMFUL.

ONE WAY TO MAKE A DENT IN THIS PROBLEM IS TO PARTICIPATE IN OR ORGANIZE A *WIKIPEDIA* EDIT-A-THON THAT COULD NOT ONLY RECRUIT AND TRAIN NEW *WIKIPEDIA* EDITORS BUT COULD IMPROVE AND EXPAND CONTENT IN AREAS THAT NEED ATTENTION. ART+FEMINISM (www.artandfeminism.org) IS A GREAT EXAMPLE OF AN ORGANIZATION THAT WORKS TO HOST EDIT-A-THONS AND CONNECT PEOPLE WHO ARE INTERESTED IN IMPROVING *WIKIPEDIA*.*

*LEARN MORE ABOUT HOW TO RUN AN EDIT-A-THON AT *https://en.wikipedia.org/wiki/Wikipedia:How_to_run_an_edit-a-thon*. AND GET THE BASICS ON HOW TO BE A PROFICIENT USER AND EDITOR AT *https://dashboard.wikiedu.org/training/students*.

CRITICAL THINKING EXERCISES

1. Search Google, Bing, or DuckDuckGo using the search statement(s) you've developed for your topic. How many results do you get? Scroll through the first 5–10 pages and note how many results on each page seem to be relevant for your research.

2. Use Google's Advanced Search to search for your topic. Which tools did you try? How did they impact your results? How does this compare to an advanced search in a library database for the same topic?

3. Identify a government, educational, professional, or public organization that provides information or does research related to your topic. Browse their website for information about them. What sites can you identify that might be useful for your research? How?

4. Look for *Wikipedia*'s guidelines for writing and editing pages. Explain the process in your own words. How does this change your perception of *Wikipedia* and how you will use the site going forward?

5. Find an article on the web that addresses algorithmic bias in a specific area. (Some ideas: education, law enforcement, job applications, web searching, home ownership, etc.) Describe who the bias impacts, what design decisions led to the bias, and why it is important to find solutions to the problem.

6. Find a *Wikipedia* article relevant to your topic. How can you use this article to expand your search for information?

CHAPTER SIX
EVALUATING YOUR SOURCES

WE'VE ALLUDED TO THAT A NUMBER OF TIMES, BUT WE HAVEN'T REALLY TALKED ABOUT HOW TO DETERMINE IF A SOURCE IS WORTH USING IN YOUR RESEARCH. THERE ARE GOOD SOURCES, BAD SOURCES, AND IN-BETWEEN SOURCES. AND THE QUALITY OF THOSE SOURCES CAN SHIFT DEPENDING ON THE CONTEXT OF YOUR OWN NEEDS.

NOT ALL INFORMATION IS EQUAL.

SO LET'S TALK ABOUT HOW TO EFFECTIVELY EXAMINE A SOURCE AND JUDGE THE QUALITY OF ITS INFORMATION.

THIS PROCESS CAN BE RELATIVE: DEPENDING ON YOUR RESEARCH TOPIC AND THE APPROACH YOU'RE TAKING, A SOURCE CAN BE EITHER GOOD **OR** BAD; **MORE** USEFUL OR **LESS** USEFUL.

FOR EXAMPLE, IF I'M STUDYING THE LOCAL, STATE, AND FEDERAL AUTHORITIES' PUBLIC RESPONSES TO A NATURAL DISASTER, THE GENERAL PUBLIC'S TWITTER RESPONSES WON'T NECESSARILY PROVIDE THE INFORMATION I NEED. I COULD LOOK AT THE RELEVANT GOVERNMENT WEBSITES AND MAYBE EVEN **THEIR** TWITTER FEEDS FOR USEFUL INFORMATION.

IF, HOWEVER, I WANT TO RESEARCH HOW INFORMATION (OR MISINFORMATION) GENERALLY SPREADS VIA TWITTER DURING THAT DISASTER, I WOULD DEFINITELY WANT TO INCLUDE THE TWEETS OF THE GENERAL PUBLIC IN MY STUDY.

IN THE FIRST CASE, THE INFORMATION FOUND IN THOSE CIVILIAN TWEETS MAY NOT BE RELEVANT, BUT A CHANGE IN PERSPECTIVE SUDDENLY MADE THEM POTENTIALLY USEFUL.

EXAMINE EACH SOURCE YOU USE, WHETHER IT'S FROM AN ACADEMIC JOURNAL, POPULAR MAGAZINE, BOOK, WEBSITE, OR A PERSON YELLING ON THE STREET CORNER. EVERY PIECE OF INFORMATION NEEDS TO BE EVALUATED; THERE ARE MULTIPLE FACTORS CONTRIBUTING TO A SOURCE'S USEFULNESS.

EVALUATING INFORMATION ISN'T JUST IMPORTANT FOR SCHOOL RESEARCH.

HIGH-QUALITY INFORMATION CAN HELP YOU DECIDE WHAT CAR TO PURCHASE OR WHICH DOCTOR TO SEE. BEING A CRITICAL USER OF INFORMATION CAN HELP YOU BE MORE USEFUL AND PRODUCTIVE IN YOUR JOB. YOU MAY NEED TO RESEARCH THE COMPETITION OR FIGURE OUT HOW TO SOLVE A LEGAL QUESTION. KNOWING HOW TO TELL GOOD INFORMATION FROM BAD CAN BE A MAJOR FACTOR IN YOUR OVERALL SUCCESS.

BEING AN ACTIVE AND EFFECTIVE CITIZEN REQUIRES YOU TO BE INFORMED. THERE IS A LOT OF MISINFORMATION OUT THERE TO LEAD YOU ASTRAY. BEING ABLE TO EXAMINE THE QUALITY OF INFORMATION HELPS YOU BECOME MORE ABLE TO ACT—AND VOTE—IN AN EDUCATED, RESPONSIBLE MANNER.

WE WANT TO SHOW YOU ANOTHER WAY TO CONSIDER EVALUATING INFORMATION ONLINE— A METHOD THAT FOCUSES ON VERIFYING INFORMATION FROM MULTIPLE SOURCES, LIKE AN INVESTIGATIVE REPORTER, AND MAKING SURE ALL YOUR SOURCES AGREE. IF THEY DON'T, YOU CAN FIGURE OUT WHY BY EXPLORING THE CONTEXT SURROUNDING THE INFORMATION.

THE METHOD WE'RE GOING TO SHOW YOU WAS DEVELOPED BY EDUCATOR MIKE CAULFIELD.* IT IS INTENDED TO HELP YOU FACT-CHECK THE INFORMATION YOU FIND ONLINE BY USING FOUR STEPS, WHICH YOU CAN REMEMBER WITH ONE SIMPLE WORD:

*WHO HAS PUBLISHED A BOOK, Web Literacy for Student Fact-Checkers (https://webliteracy.pressbooks.com/) AND KEEPS A BLOG (https://hapgood.us/) ABOUT HIS WORK.

STEP ONE:

 Aunt Petunia shared:
PUBLIC

 PatriotEagleHealthNews.ru

THIS ONE WEIRD TRICK WILL LET YOU AVOID ALL VACCINES FOR LIFE!

~~~~ *anger!* ~~~~ *fear!* ~~~~ ~~ ~~~~ *click!* ~~ ~~ *buy! buy! buy!* ~~ ~~~~ ~~~~ ~~ ~~~~ ~~~~ ~~ ~~~~

 AD

I KNOW, I KNOW, WE'VE BARELY STARTED. WHEN YOU FIRST ENCOUNTER A NEW PIECE OF INFORMATION, BE IT A TWEET, A WEBSITE, A PHOTO, A NEWS STORY, OR SOMETHING ELSE, BEFORE YOU DO ANYTHING, STOP, AND PAY ATTENTION TO THE CONTEXT AROUND THIS INFORMATION.

HOW DID YOU FIND IT?

WHO SHARED IT WITH YOU?

WHAT DO YOU KNOW ABOUT THEM?

DID THE INFORMATION PROVOKE A STRONG EMOTIONAL RESPONSE? DOES IT MAKE YOU HAPPY? ANGRY? SAD? OUR JUDGMENT CAN OFTEN BE CLOUDED BY EMOTIONS, AND WE MAY BE MORE LIKELY TO BELIEVE OR SHARE SOMETHING THAT TRIGGERS A RESPONSE WITHOUT TAKING EVEN 30 SECONDS TO MAKE A QUICK INVESTIGATION.

SO STOP, THINK, PAY ATTENTION TO HOW YOU FEEL, BE AWARE OF YOUR INITIAL REACTION, AND PLAN TO GAIN MORE CONTEXT BEFORE MOVING ON.

STEP TWO:
INVESTIGATE THE SOURCE

WITH ANY PIECE OF INFORMATION, YOU WANT TO KNOW WHO IS RESPONSIBLE FOR IT. IS IT FROM A REPUTABLE NEWS ORGANIZATION? IS IT A WELL-KNOWN, TRUSTED WEBSITE? MAYBE A RESPECTED RESEARCHER?

OR IS IT FROM A WEBSITE KNOWN FOR SPREADING HYPERPARTISAN OR MALICIOUS CONTENT?

WHO HAS CREATED IT AND WHY ARE THEY QUALIFIED TO COMMENT ON THE ISSUE?

YOU MIGHT NOT RECOGNIZE THE SOURCE OF THE INFORMATION YOU FOUND, THOUGH, IN WHICH CASE A LITTLE INVESTIGATIVE WORK IS NEEDED.* YOU CAN START BY DOING A GOOGLE OR A *WIKIPEDIA* SEARCH FOR INFORMATION ABOUT THE WEBSITE YOU FOUND, OR ABOUT THE AUTHOR OF A PARTICULAR ARTICLE OR POST. IT'S VITAL TO **GET OUT OF** THE ORIGINAL SOURCE AND SEE WHAT OTHERS HAVE TO SAY ABOUT IT.

THIS SITE DOESN'T FACT-CHECK!

AND THEY HAVE A WELL-KNOWN BIAS AGAINST EXCLAMATION MARKS.

*EVEN IF YOU RECOGNIZE WHERE THE CONTENT IS FROM AND TRUST IT, YOU SHOULD CHECK YOUR OWN BIAS AND CONSIDER WHY **YOU** TRUST A SOURCE. IS IT BECAUSE THEY HAVE GOOD PRACTICES OR BECAUSE YOU **WANT** TO BELIEVE WHAT THEY WRITE?

REMEMBER, TOO, THAT JUST BECAUSE SOMETHING HAS A BIAS DOES NOT AUTOMATICALLY MEAN THE INFORMATION ISN'T LEGITIMATE. **BUT** IF THE RESEARCH WAS PAID FOR, SPONSORED, OR OTHERWISE INFLUENCED BY SOMEONE WHO HAS AN INTEREST IN HOW THAT RESEARCH TURNS OUT, YOU SHOULD BE MADE AWARE OF THAT POTENTIAL CONFLICT OF INTEREST. A GOOD SOURCE WILL TELL YOU WHEN THAT CONFLICT EXISTS.

A NEW RESEARCH STUDY FINDS THAT UNIVERSITIES WITH TERRIFYING MASCOTS WIN SIGNIFICANTLY MORE SPORTSBALL GAMES THAN THOSE WITHOUT.

STEP THREE:
FIND MORE (OR BETTER) COVERAGE

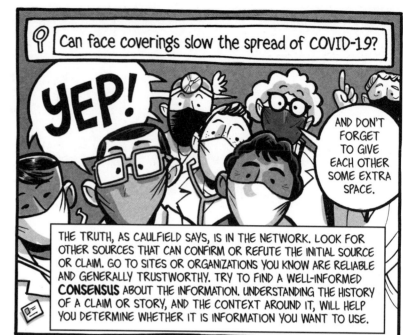

Can face coverings slow the spread of COVID-19?

YEP!

AND DON'T FORGET TO GIVE EACH OTHER SOME EXTRA SPACE.

THE TRUTH, AS CAULFIELD SAYS, IS IN THE NETWORK. LOOK FOR OTHER SOURCES THAT CAN CONFIRM OR REFUTE THE INITIAL SOURCE OR CLAIM. GO TO SITES OR ORGANIZATIONS YOU KNOW ARE RELIABLE AND GENERALLY TRUSTWORTHY. TRY TO FIND A WELL-INFORMED **CONSENSUS** ABOUT THE INFORMATION. UNDERSTANDING THE HISTORY OF A CLAIM OR STORY, AND THE CONTEXT AROUND IT, WILL HELP YOU DETERMINE WHETHER IT IS INFORMATION YOU WANT TO USE.

REMEMBER THAT YOU'RE NOT THE ONLY ONE INTERESTED IN MAKING SURE THAT INFORMATION IS ACCURATE. YOU CAN RELY ON THE WORK OF ESTABLISHED FACT-CHECKING ORGANIZATIONS AND SAVE SOME TIME. Snopes.com, Factcheck.org, AND Politifact.com ARE ALL EXCELLENT STARTING POINTS FOR FIGURING OUT IF SOMETHING IS TRUE, FALSE, OR JUST MORE COMPLICATED THAN IT ORIGINALLY SEEMED.

THESE SITES ALSO PROVIDE TONS OF EVIDENCE, LINKING BACK TO A VARIETY OF ORIGINAL SOURCES AND OFFERING BROADER CONTEXT TO HELP YOU BETTER UNDERSTAND THE ISSUE.

UH OH. HEY. DID GENETICALLY MODIFIED TOMATOES REALLY KILL SOMEONE?

ON IT!

STEP FOUR:
TRACE CLAIMS, QUOTES, AND MEDIA BACK TO THEIR ORIGINAL CONTEXT

Peer-reviewed research paper declares that Vaccines Cause Autism...

...but we're not going to tell you that the original research done for this single study was fundamentally flawed, ethically atrocious, and eventually retracted by the medical journal, because that's not going to get clicks, so...

A LOT OF WHAT WE FIND ONLINE IS TAKEN OUT OF CONTEXT OR ONLY TELLS PART OF THE STORY. A CLIP FROM AN INTERVIEW MIGHT BE SHARED, FOR EXAMPLE, MAKING IT SOUND LIKE SOMEONE SAID ONE THING, WHEN THEY ACTUALLY SAID THE OPPOSITE.

IMAGES, VIDEOS, AND QUOTES CAN BE CROPPED, SNIPPED, AND FAKED, MAKING IT HARD FOR PEOPLE TO KNOW WHAT IS TRUE AND WHAT IS MISLEADING. IN THESE CASES, IT IS IMPORTANT TO TRACE THOSE THINGS BACK TO THEIR ORIGINAL CONTEXT—IF YOU CAN—SO YOU CAN DETERMINE IF THEY ARE ACCURATELY REPRESENTED OR IF THEY ARE BEING MISUSED.

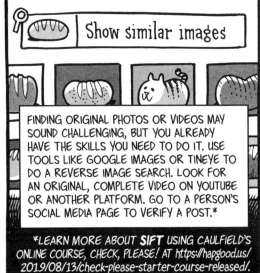

Show similar images

FINDING ORIGINAL PHOTOS OR VIDEOS MAY SOUND CHALLENGING, BUT YOU ALREADY HAVE THE SKILLS YOU NEED TO DO IT. USE TOOLS LIKE GOOGLE IMAGES OR TINEYE TO DO A REVERSE IMAGE SEARCH. LOOK FOR AN ORIGINAL, COMPLETE VIDEO ON YOUTUBE OR ANOTHER PLATFORM. GO TO A PERSON'S SOCIAL MEDIA PAGE TO VERIFY A POST.*

*LEARN MORE ABOUT **SIFT** USING CAULFIELD'S ONLINE COURSE, CHECK, PLEASE! AT https://hapgood.us/2019/08/13/check-please-starter-course-released/.

THINK ABOUT WHERE THAT ORIGINAL CONTENT MIGHT BE LOCATED, AND WHAT SEARCH TERMS WILL GET YOU THERE THE FASTEST. USE THOSE RESEARCH SKILLS YOU DEVELOPED IN EARLIER CHAPTERS TO DIG DOWN UNTIL YOU FEEL CONFIDENT THAT YOU HAVE FOUND THE GOOD STUFF. IF YOU TAKE THE TIME TO DO THIS, YOU'RE LIKELY TO MAKE BETTER DECISIONS AND MAY EVEN HELP STOP THE SPREAD OF BAD INFORMATION.

Look at this article! 5G Cell Tower Radiation Activates COVID-19 in Your Body!

Study: COVID-19 fear-mongering proves big business for anyone lacking moral compass

Pundit reads tweet on air from Twitter user @DefinitelyRealPerson10641 questioning safety of 5G

Int'l Commission on Non-Ionizing Radiation Protection Notes That 5G Exposure Should Not Cause Human Harm, Provided Appropriate Restrictions*

*https://www.icnirp.org/en/applications/5g/index.html

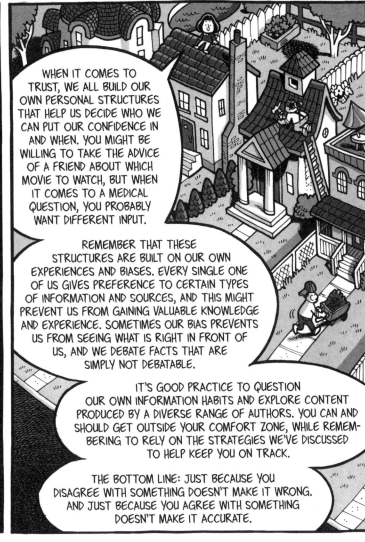

WHEN IT COMES TO TRUST, WE ALL BUILD OUR OWN PERSONAL STRUCTURES THAT HELP US DECIDE WHO WE CAN PUT OUR CONFIDENCE IN AND WHEN. YOU MIGHT BE WILLING TO TAKE THE ADVICE OF A FRIEND ABOUT WHICH MOVIE TO WATCH, BUT WHEN IT COMES TO A MEDICAL QUESTION, YOU PROBABLY WANT DIFFERENT INPUT.

REMEMBER THAT THESE STRUCTURES ARE BUILT ON OUR OWN EXPERIENCES AND BIASES. EVERY SINGLE ONE OF US GIVES PREFERENCE TO CERTAIN TYPES OF INFORMATION AND SOURCES, AND THIS MIGHT PREVENT US FROM GAINING VALUABLE KNOWLEDGE AND EXPERIENCE. SOMETIMES OUR BIAS PREVENTS US FROM SEEING WHAT IS RIGHT IN FRONT OF US, AND WE DEBATE FACTS THAT ARE SIMPLY NOT DEBATABLE.

IT'S GOOD PRACTICE TO QUESTION OUR OWN INFORMATION HABITS AND EXPLORE CONTENT PRODUCED BY A DIVERSE RANGE OF AUTHORS. YOU CAN AND SHOULD GET OUTSIDE YOUR COMFORT ZONE, WHILE REMEMBERING TO RELY ON THE STRATEGIES WE'VE DISCUSSED TO HELP KEEP YOU ON TRACK.

THE BOTTOM LINE: JUST BECAUSE YOU DISAGREE WITH SOMETHING DOESN'T MAKE IT WRONG. AND JUST BECAUSE YOU AGREE WITH SOMETHING DOESN'T MAKE IT ACCURATE.

A FINAL, FUNDAMENTAL QUESTION YOU SHOULD ASK ABOUT A SOURCE IS, DOES IT CONTRIBUTE TO YOUR WORK? IS IT SOMETHING YOU CAN USE FOR YOUR RESEARCH, OR IS IT BETTER LEFT OUT?

HOW **RELEVANT** IS THE SOURCE TO YOUR RESEARCH? OBVIOUSLY, A BOOK ON ABRAHAM LINCOLN WON'T BE RELEVANT TO A RESEARCH PROJECT ON THE PHYSICS OF BASEBALL.

WELL, **PROBABLY** NOT, ANYWAY.

FOUR RUNS AND SEVEN INNINGS AGO...

SOMETIMES IT'S MORE COMPLICATED AND NUANCED THAN THAT. A MORE PRECISE QUESTION MIGHT BE, HOW DIRECTLY DOES THE SOURCE ADDRESS YOUR OWN RESEARCH?

ANOTHER WAY TO GAUGE RELEVANCE IS TO EXAMINE HOW MUCH OVERLAP A SOURCE SHARES WITH YOUR TOPIC. ABE LINCOLN AND BASEBALL PHYSICS HAVE ZERO OVERLAP, BUT AN ARTICLE ON FREQUENT EXERCISE FOR OLDER PERSONS MIGHT BE AN EXCELLENT FIT FOR, SAY, RESEARCHING WHAT FACTORS HELP PEOPLE LIVE LONGER.

YOU SHOULD ALSO CHECK THE SOURCE'S **CURRENCY:** HOW RECENTLY IT WAS CREATED OR UPDATED. IN MANY CASES, YOU WANT INFORMATION AS CURRENT AS POSSIBLE, SINCE SUCH SOURCES LIKELY INCLUDE THE MOST UP-TO-DATE RESEARCH. THIS IS ESPECIALLY TRUE FOR TECHNOLOGY, MEDICINE, OR OTHER RAPIDLY CHANGING FIELDS, BUT MAY NOT MATTER AS MUCH WHEN STUDYING CERTAIN HISTORICAL TOPICS.

↑ SURGERY VS. SURGERY ↓

↑ COMPUTER VS. COMPUTER ↓

ALWAYS CHECK TO SEE IF YOUR SOURCE IS DATED AND THEN DETERMINE WHETHER OR NOT IT MATTERS BY LOOKING AT OTHER SOURCES ON THE SAME TOPIC. SEE IF RECENT MATERIALS HAVE RENDERED THE OLD STUFF OBSOLETE.

CRITICAL THINKING EXERCISES

1. Locate a general website that is relevant to your research topic. Try to choose one that is unfamiliar to you. Choose one claim the website makes, and evaluate it using the SIFT steps. Describe your process of completing each step. When you have completed your evaluation, reflect on the entire process: Which parts were easy or challenging? What is your final assessment of the source you found?

2. Identify a good, potentially relevant source on the open web. Write a brief summary of the source (two or three sentences), and describe how that source contributes to your research and understanding of your topic.

3. What kind of "information bias" do you have? Are you more likely to access, consume, and believe content made available through certain media? Do your preferences change depending on your information need? How so? Identify some types of information you knowingly avoid and attempt to assess why you feel a certain way about that info. Take time to evaluate the source(s) and try to imagine possible scenarios in which that particular information would be relevant to someone. Do you feel that your preferences are justified, or have you discovered new potential sources of useful information?

4. How do you feel about using information that you find through Facebook, Twitter, and other social media in your own research? How could you determine the authority of an author who posts something online through social media?

5. Is your research topic dependent on the most up-to-date information and research? Why or why not?

CHAPTER SEVEN
USING INFORMATION ETHICALLY

PLAGIARISM
CITATION

A LOT OF STUDENTS HEAR THE TERMS **PLAGIARISM** AND **CITATION** AND IMMEDIATELY COLLAPSE IN GIBBERING, INCOHERENT TERROR. YOU DON'T NEED TO BE SCARED. THE SUBJECT'S A **LOT** LESS COMPLICATED THAN YOU THINK.

FIRST OF ALL, LET'S DEFINE THE TERMS.

PLAGIARISM
IS THE ACT OF TAKING SOMEONE ELSE'S WORK AND USING IT AS YOUR OWN, WITHOUT GIVING CREDIT TO THOSE WHO ACTUALLY DID THE RESEARCH AND WRITING.

RESEARCH

IT'S INTELLECTUAL THIEVERY. SIMPLY PUT, IT'S STEALING.

SO, HOW DO YOU REFER TO SOMEONE ELSE'S WORK WITHOUT PLAGIARIZING IT? WHAT TORTUOUS AND CONVOLUTED PROCESS MUST YOU GO THROUGH TO ENSURE THAT YOUR WORK IS YOUR OWN AND THAT YOU'RE NOT ACCUSED OF STEALING?

IT'S ACTUALLY VERY, VERY SIMPLE: **GIVE CREDIT WHERE CREDIT IS DUE.**

THIS IS CALLED **CITATION.**

REMEMBER, RESEARCH IS A COLLECTIVE PROCESS. AS A RESEARCHER, YOU CONTRIBUTE TO THE PROCESS BY BUILDING ON THE WORK OF OTHERS. YOU'RE NOT DOING ANYTHING WRONG BY USING THIS RESEARCH. THAT'S THE **POINT!** THE BODY OF RESEARCH GROWS THROUGH THE YEARS BECAUSE PEOPLE REACH NEW CONCLUSIONS AND MAKE NEW DISCOVERIES, EACH ONE BUILT OFF OF ITS PREDECESSORS IN SOME WAY.

RESEARCH

RESEARCH

USING THE WORK OF OTHERS IS OK. IN FACT, YOU KIND OF HAVE TO... OTHERWISE YOU START FROM SCRATCH.

YOU JUST HAVE TO REMEMBER TO **GIVE CREDIT.**

NOW, LET'S SAY I DECIDE I CAN TELL STEVE'S STORY A LITTLE BETTER, SO I PUT THE STORY INTO MY OWN WORDS. FOR EXAMPLE...

MY PARACHUTE FAILED AS I FELL FROM THE PLANE. THE GROUND APPROACHED AT AN INCREDIBLE RATE, AND THE WIND ROARED IN MY EARS...

YOU MIGHT THINK I'VE DONE A NICE JOB OF MAKING THE STORY MY OWN, BUT GUESS WHO'S STILL MAD?

SEE, THAT WAS **STILL** PLAGIARIZING BECAUSE EVEN THOUGH I DIDN'T USE THE EXACT WORDS THAT STEVE USED, I TOOK THE IDEA AND MADE IT SEEM LIKE IT WAS MY OWN.

SORRY, STEVE. I WAS JUST MAKING A POINT...

I WANT OUT OF THIS EXAMPLE, NOW!

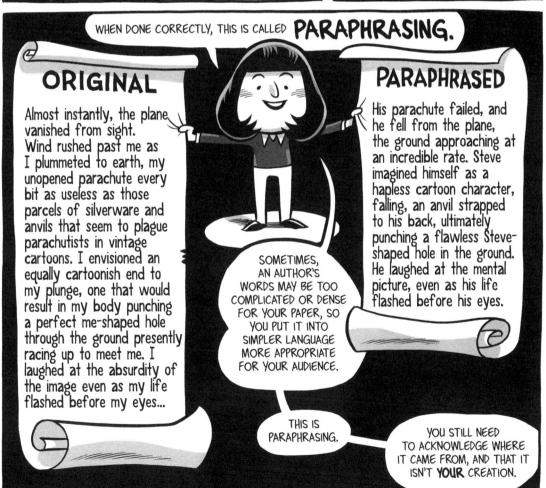

WHEN DONE CORRECTLY, THIS IS CALLED **PARAPHRASING.**

ORIGINAL

Almost instantly, the plane vanished from sight. Wind rushed past me as I plummeted to earth, my unopened parachute every bit as useless as those parcels of silverware and anvils that seem to plague parachutists in vintage cartoons. I envisioned an equally cartoonish end to my plunge, one that would result in my body punching a perfect me-shaped hole through the ground presently racing up to meet me. I laughed at the absurdity of the image even as my life flashed before my eyes...

PARAPHRASED

His parachute failed, and he fell from the plane, the ground approaching at an incredible rate. Steve imagined himself as a hapless cartoon character, falling, an anvil strapped to his back, ultimately punching a flawless Steve-shaped hole in the ground. He laughed at the mental picture, even as his life flashed before his eyes.

SOMETIMES, AN AUTHOR'S WORDS MAY BE TOO COMPLICATED OR DENSE FOR YOUR PAPER, SO YOU PUT IT INTO SIMPLER LANGUAGE MORE APPROPRIATE FOR YOUR AUDIENCE.

THIS IS PARAPHRASING.

YOU STILL NEED TO ACKNOWLEDGE WHERE IT CAME FROM, AND THAT IT ISN'T **YOUR** CREATION.

NOW, IF YOU DIGEST AND CONDENSE AN IDEA, THAT'S CALLED **SUMMARIZING**. YOU USE YOUR OWN WORDS TO EXPLAIN ANOTHER PERSON'S RESEARCH IN A FEW SENTENCES, WITHOUT DIRECTLY QUOTING OR PARAPHRASING THEM.

YOU CAN TAKE MULTIPLE IDEAS FROM A SOURCE AND COMPRESS THEM INTO SOMETHING YOUR AUDIENCE CAN READ QUICKLY AND UNDERSTAND.

AUTHOR'S VERSION:

Almost instantly, the plane vanished from sight. Wind rushed past me as I plummeted to earth, my unopened parachute every bit as useless as those parcels of silverware and anvils that seem to plague parachutists in vintage cartoons. I envisioned an equally cartoonish end to my plunge, one that would result in my body punching a perfect me-shaped hole through the ground presently racing up to meet me. I laughed at the absurdity of the image even as my life flashed before my eyes...

SUMMARY:

Steve's parachute didn't open. He imagined himself as a cartoon character, complete with an anvil on his back and leaving a perfect Steve-shaped hole in the ground. The image made him laugh in spite of his impending demise.

NOW, NOT QUITE EVERYTHING NEEDS A CITATION. IF YOU HAVE FACTS IN YOUR PAPER THAT ARE COMMON KNOWLEDGE, THOSE FACTS DON'T REQUIRE CITATIONS.

FOR EXAMPLE, IF YOU SAY WORLD WAR II RESULTED IN THE DEATHS OF MILLIONS OF PEOPLE AROUND THE GLOBE, YOU DON'T NEED A CITATION. THAT'S COMMON KNOWLEDGE.

IF, HOWEVER, YOU WANT TO INCLUDE A SPECIFIC NUMBER OF DEATHS, YOU'LL NEED TO CITE WHERE YOU GOT THAT FIGURE, SINCE THERE ARE DIFFERENT ESTIMATES IN DIFFERENT SOURCES.

To my buddy, Steve. Sorry, Dude.

AS A RESEARCHER, YOU ARE (OR SHOULD BE) CREATING NEW KNOWLEDGE BY **SYNTHESIZING** THE VARIETY OF INFORMATION YOU'VE ENCOUNTERED INTO A NEW PRODUCT.

SURE, YOU'RE USING **EXISTING** RESEARCH AND INFORMATION, BUT YOU MAY BRING UNIQUE UNDERSTANDING AND EXPERIENCE TO THE TABLE THAT HELPS DEFINE THE NEW WORK AS YOUR OWN.

THE FINAL PRODUCT SHOULD BE YOUR OWN CREATION, YOUR OWN UNDERSTANDING OF HOW ALL THE PIECES COME TOGETHER. YOU'RE NOT SIMPLY LISTING OR SUMMARIZING ALL THE OTHER RESEARCH OUT THERE. YOU'RE BUILDING A NEW UNDERSTANDING OF THAT RESEARCH AND CONTRIBUTING TO THE CONVERSATION!

TO SUM UP, IF YOU TAKE SOMEONE'S EXACT WORDS, OR EXPRESS THEIR IDEAS IN YOUR OWN WORDS, AND DON'T GIVE CREDIT, YOU'RE GUILTY OF PLAGIARISM. SO DON'T DO THAT!

HERE'S ANOTHER TIP: KEEP TRACK OF YOUR SOURCES AS YOU WORK.

IT'S ENTIRELY TOO EASY TO LOSE TRACK OF WHAT SOURCES YOU WANT TO USE IF YOU DON'T, AND TRYING TO CITE EVERYTHING AT THE LAST MINUTE IS A RECIPE FOR DISASTER, SINCE YOU'RE MORE LIKELY TO FORGET WHO WROTE WHAT, AS WELL AS WHAT YOU'VE QUOTED, PARAPHRASED, OR SUMMARIZED.

AT THE VERY LEAST, WRITE DOWN WHAT SOURCES YOU'RE USING SO YOU CAN REFER BACK TO THEM. IDEALLY, YOU CAN USE SOMETHING CALLED A **CITATION MANAGER** TO KEEP TRACK OF YOUR SOURCES ONLINE.

YOUR SCHOOL MIGHT SUBSCRIBE TO ONE. THERE ARE SOME GOOD FREE OPTIONS OUT THERE TOO, LIKE ZOTERO,* SO BE SURE TO CHECK THOSE OUT.

THEY CAN SAVE YOU A LOT OF TIME AND HASSLE WHEN IT COMES TO ORGANIZING YOUR SOURCES AND WILL HELP YOU AVOID INADVERTENTLY USING A SOURCE WITHOUT CITING IT.

Bibliography

*www.zotero.org OR zbib.org FOR A MORE BASIC VERSION

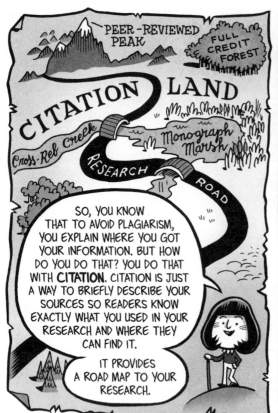

SO, YOU KNOW THAT TO AVOID PLAGIARISM, YOU EXPLAIN WHERE YOU GOT YOUR INFORMATION. BUT HOW DO YOU DO THAT? YOU DO THAT WITH **CITATION**. CITATION IS JUST A WAY TO BRIEFLY DESCRIBE YOUR SOURCES SO READERS KNOW EXACTLY WHAT YOU USED IN YOUR RESEARCH AND WHERE THEY CAN FIND IT.

IT PROVIDES A ROAD MAP TO YOUR RESEARCH.

CITATIONS ARE AN EXAMPLE OF HOW NEW RESEARCH BUILDS ON OLDER RESEARCH. YOU CAN LOOK AT A BOOK OR ARTICLE AND TELL WHAT SOURCES THAT AUTHOR USED IN ORDER TO REACH THEIR OWN CONCLUSIONS. THINK OF RESEARCH AS AN ONGOING, NEVERENDING, ALWAYS-CHANGING **CONVERSATION**.

THERE ARE MANY VOICES AND VIEWPOINTS THAT CONTRIBUTE TO THE DISCUSSION, INCLUDING YOUR OWN! BE SURE TO ACT AS A RESPONSIBLE AND ETHICAL PARTICIPANT BY BEING HONEST WITH YOUR RESEARCH AND CITING THE WORK OF OTHERS.

NOT ONLY DO CITATIONS KEEP YOU OUT OF TROUBLE—THE CITATIONS IN EACH OF YOUR SOURCES CAN ALSO HELP YOU FIND RESOURCES FOR YOUR OWN RESEARCH!

LET'S SAY YOU USE A LIBRARY SEARCH OR DATABASE TO LOCATE A REALLY GOOD BOOK OR ARTICLE, BUT YOU DON'T FIND ANYTHING ELSE IN YOUR SEARCH RESULTS. WELL, **FLIP OR SCROLL TO THE END** OF THAT SOURCE.

THERE YOU'LL FIND THE LIST OF SOURCES THE AUTHOR USED, CALLED A BIBLIOGRAPHY, WORKS CITED, OR REFERENCES. THIS CAN BE A GOLD MINE! YOU MIGHT HAVE HUNDREDS OF POTENTIALLY USEFUL ITEMS LISTED FOR YOU RIGHT THERE! ALL YOU HAVE TO DO IS FIND THEM.

THEY MIGHT BE IN YOUR LIBRARY OR ITS DATABASES, OR YOU MIGHT HAVE TO REQUEST THEM FROM ANOTHER LIBRARY THROUGH INTERLIBRARY LOAN. THE POINT IS, SOMEONE HAS ALREADY DONE A TON OF RESEARCH ON YOUR TOPIC. BUILD ON WHAT THEY HAVE DONE, AND TRACK DOWN THE SOURCES THEY USED FOR THEIR RESEARCH.

WHO KNOWS, YOU MAY DISCOVER SOMETHING THAT THEY MISSED!

LIKE OTHER CONVERSATIONS, RESEARCH CAN BE EXCLUSIVE AND LEAVE SOME VOICES OUT, INTENTIONALLY OR NOT.

AT FIRST, YOU MAY FEEL THAT YOUR VOICE IS A RELATIVELY MINOR ONE IN THE CONVERSATION, AND MAYBE FOR GOOD REASON. YOU'RE JUST LEARNING ABOUT A TOPIC AND ABOUT THE RESEARCH PROCESS.

OTHERS WITH MORE EXPERIENCE, LIKE YOUR PROFESSORS, CAN AND SHOULD HELP YOU DEVELOP YOUR VOICE AND ABILITY TO CONTRIBUTE IN MEANINGFUL WAYS. IT'S A PROCESS, AND YOUR CONFIDENCE AND ABILITY WILL IMPROVE.

ON THE OTHER HAND, RESEARCH CAN OFTEN FEEL CLOSED OFF FOR FAR LESS LEGITIMATE REASONS. WHO TENDS TO BE CITED AND WHY? WHO TENDS TO BE PUBLISHED AND WHY? WHEN YOU EXAMINE THE CITATIONS IN A SOURCE, YOU'RE LOOKING AT A HISTORY OF DECISIONS MADE BY PUBLISHERS AND AUTHORS ABOUT WHO GETS TO BE A PART OF THE LARGER SCHOLARLY CONVERSATION AND, HISTORICALLY, IT'S BEEN DOMINATED BY WHITE MEN. IMPORTANT PIECES OF THE CONVERSATION ARE MISSING, AND WE'RE THE WORSE FOR IT.

A GOOD DEAL OF RESEARCH ACROSS A VARIETY OF DISCIPLINES* SHOWS THAT WOMEN AND PEOPLE OF COLOR HAVE OFTEN BEEN EXCLUDED FROM THE CONVERSATION AND HAVE CONTINUALLY BEEN UNDERREPRESENTED WHEN IT COMES TO HOW OFTEN THEY ARE PUBLISHED AND HOW OFTEN THEIR WORK IS CITED. THIS UNDERREPRESENTATION JUST SERVES TO REINFORCE THE PERCEPTION THAT WOMEN AND PEOPLE OF COLOR ARE NOT PRODUCING SIGNIFICANT RESEARCH.

TO COMBAT THIS, YOU CAN WORK TO INTENTIONALLY SEEK OUT, READ, AND CITE THE WORK OF THOSE WHOSE VOICES HAVE BEEN SILENCED IN THE PAST.**

*TO LIST JUST A FEW:

"#CommunicationSoWhite" by P. Chakravartty, R. Kuo, V. Grubbs, and C. McIlwain (https://doi.org/10.1093/joc/jqy003)

"Is Publishing in the Chemical Sciences Gender Biased?" by the Royal Society of Chemistry (https://www.rsc.org/new-perspectives/talent/gender-bias-in-publishing/)

"The Myth of Meritocracy in Academic Publishing" by S. Muka (https://thenewinquiry.com/blog/the-myth-of-meritocracy-in-academic-publishing/)

**SEE CITE BLACK WOMEN AT www.citeblackwomencollective.org.

FURTHERMORE, NOT ALL RESEARCHERS HAVE ACCESS TO THE SAME RESOURCES. THOSE WHO DON'T HAVE THE PRIVILEGE OF WORKING AT A SCHOOL OR ORGANIZATION THAT CAN PAY FOR ACCESS TO RESEARCH THROUGH DATABASES AND JOURNAL SUBSCRIPTIONS ARE BASICALLY LOCKED OUT, TRYING TO PIECE TOGETHER THE CONVERSATION JUST BY CATCHING SNIPPETS OF WHAT'S GOING ON.

YOU MAY HAVE MORE ACCESS TO RESOURCES AS A COLLEGE STUDENT THAN A PROFESSIONAL RESEARCHER AT ANOTHER INSTITUTION. THIS IS WHY OPEN ACCESS IS SO IMPORTANT TO GLOBAL RESEARCH!

RESEARCH PAPERS CAN BE WRITTEN IN A VARIETY OF "STYLES." THERE ARE MULTIPLE STYLE MANUALS, EACH OFFERING DIFFERENT GUIDELINES FOR WRITING RESEARCH PAPERS.

MLA
Humanities

APA
Social Sciences

CHICAGO
History

SOME OF THE MOST COMMON GUIDES ARE THE MLA HANDBOOK FOR WRITERS OF RESEARCH PAPERS (MODERN LANGUAGE ASSOCIATION), THE PUBLICATION MANUAL OF THE AMERICAN PSYCHOLOGICAL ASSOCIATION (APA), AND THE CHICAGO MANUAL OF STYLE (OR A VARIATION KNOWN AS TURABIAN). THESE STYLES ARE TYPICALLY ASSOCIATED WITH DIFFERENT ACADEMIC DISCIPLINES.*

THESE GUIDES PROVIDE INCREDIBLY DETAILED INSTRUCTIONS ON HOW TO WRITE AND FORMAT YOUR PAPER IN A PARTICULAR MANNER, BUT ONE AREA THAT RECEIVES A LOT OF ATTENTION IS HOW TO APPROPRIATELY CITE YOUR SOURCES OR REFERENCES. EACH CITATION STYLE LOOKS A LITTLE DIFFERENT, BUT THE PURPOSE IS THE SAME: EXPLAINING WHERE YOU GOT YOUR INFORMATION.

*NONE OF THAT IS SET IN STONE. YOU MAY FIND THAT YOUR INSTRUCTOR PREFERS A CERTAIN STYLE EVEN THOUGH IT'S NOT TYPICALLY USED IN THAT FIELD OF STUDY. AND THESE THREE AREN'T THE ONLY STYLES, BUT THEY ARE VERY TYPICAL FOR UNDERGRADUATE RESEARCH.

REGARDLESS OF STYLE, THERE ARE BASICALLY TWO MAJOR COMPONENTS WHEN IT COMES TO CITING SOURCES. ONE, A LITTLE NOTE NEXT TO EACH QUOTE, PARAPHRASE, OR SUMMARY, INDICATING WHICH SOURCE THAT INFORMATION CAME FROM, AND TWO, A LIST AT THE END OF YOUR PAPER SPECIFYING THE SOURCES YOU USED IN YOUR RESEARCH.

1. Tell us where it came from.
2. Tell us how to get to it.

THE FIRST COMPONENT TO CITING SOMETHING IS THE LITTLE NOTE EXPLAINING WHERE YOUR INFORMATION CAME FROM.

EACH TIME YOU USE INFORMATION FROM AN OUTSIDE SOURCE, YOU HAVE TO INDICATE TO YOUR READERS WHERE YOU OBTAINED THAT INFORMATION. IT'S NOT THE FULL REFERENCE... IT'S JUST A WAY TO CATCH THE READERS' ATTENTION AND MAKE SURE THEY KNOW THE INFORMATION IS FROM ANOTHER SOURCE.

DEPENDING ON THE STYLE YOU'RE USING, THIS CAN BE DONE IN A VARIETY OF WAYS.

APA IN-TEXT

Dr. Philbert Manningham's (2019) research has noted that "according to recent trends, it would not be outlandish to claim that at some point within the next ten years, human beings will become so lazy that we will devise methods to permanently attach ourselves to portable lounge furniture" (p. 216).

CHICAGO FOOTNOTE/ENDNOTE

Dr. Philbert Manningham's research has noted that "according to recent trends, it would not be outlandish to claim that at some point within the next ten years, human beings will become so lazy that we will devise methods to permanently attach ourselves to portable lounge furniture."[7]

APA AND MLA CALL THESE SHORT NOTICES "IN-TEXT CITATIONS," WHILE CHICAGO USES THE TERMS "FOOTNOTES" OR "ENDNOTES." THESE NAMES DESCRIBE WHERE THE CITATIONS FIT WITHIN THE PAPER.

IN-TEXT CITATIONS ARE PLACED WITHIN THE ACTUAL SENTENCES IN YOUR PAPER.

FOOTNOTES USE A SUPERSCRIPT NUMBER INDICATING THAT THE CITATION INFORMATION IS INCLUDED AT THE BOTTOM, OR "FOOT," OF THE PAGE. ENDNOTES ARE SIMILAR TO FOOTNOTES, BUT THE NUMBERED CITATIONS ARE AT THE END OF THE PAPER, RATHER THAN AT THE BOTTOM OF EACH PAGE.

7. Philbert Manningham, *Couch Potato: The Future of Human/Furniture Interdependence* (New York: Association for the Study of Muscle Atrophy, 2019), 216.

APA — MANNINGHAM (2019) — (p. 216)

AUTHOR → CHICAGO — MANNINGHAM ... 7

YEAR →

PAGE → 7 MANNINGHAM (2019) 216.

EACH CITATION LOOKS DIFFERENT, BUT THEY BOTH SERVE TO IDENTIFY THE AUTHOR (MANNINGHAM), THE PAGE NUMBER OF THE QUOTE OR IDEA (216), AND THE YEAR OF PUBLICATION (2019). REMEMBER, THESE EXAMPLES SIMPLY ILLUSTRATE THE MOST POPULAR METHODS OF PROVIDING A CITATION IN EACH STYLE, AND THERE ARE OTHER METHODS NOT DESCRIBED HERE.

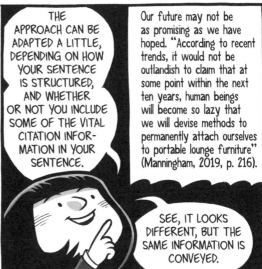

THE APPROACH CAN BE ADAPTED A LITTLE, DEPENDING ON HOW YOUR SENTENCE IS STRUCTURED, AND WHETHER OR NOT YOU INCLUDE SOME OF THE VITAL CITATION INFORMATION IN YOUR SENTENCE.

Our future may not be as promising as we have hoped. "According to recent trends, it would not be outlandish to claim that at some point within the next ten years, human beings will become so lazy that we will devise methods to permanently attach ourselves to portable lounge furniture" (Manningham, 2019, p. 216).

SEE, IT LOOKS DIFFERENT, BUT THE SAME INFORMATION IS CONVEYED.

IN-TEXT CITATIONS AND FOOTNOTES/ENDNOTES NOT ONLY TELL YOUR AUDIENCE THAT THE INFORMATION COMES FROM ANOTHER SOURCE; THEY ALSO DIRECT READERS TO THE COMPREHENSIVE LIST OF SOURCES YOU'LL INCLUDE AT THE END OF YOUR PAPER.

WORKS CITED Thataway!

THAT LIST MUST INCLUDE ALL THE SOURCES YOU'VE USED IN YOUR RESEARCH. THE LIST HAS A DIFFERENT NAME DEPENDING ON WHAT STYLE YOU'RE USING. APA TITLES IT "REFERENCES," MLA CALLS IT "WORKS CITED," WHILE CHICAGO STYLE USES THE TERM "BIBLIOGRAPHY." WITHIN EACH LIST, NOTE EVERY SINGLE SOURCE YOU USED WHILE WRITING YOUR PAPER. THESE SOURCES ARE ORGANIZED ALPHABETICALLY BY THE AUTHOR'S LAST NAME. EACH STYLE PROVIDES A PARTICULAR STRUCTURE FOR ORGANIZING THE INFORMATION ABOUT YOUR SOURCE.

References   Works Cited   Bibliography

APA   MLA   CHICAGO

EACH STYLE PUTS CITATION DATA IN A DIFFERENT ORDER AND USES DIFFERENT INDICATORS (LIKE QUOTATION MARKS, ITALICS, AND OTHER PUNCTUATION) TO KEEP THE PARTS OF THE CITATION SEPARATE. AND EACH TYPE OF SOURCE (BOOK, ARTICLE, WEBSITE, ETC.) WILL BE CITED A BIT DIFFERENTLY, AS WELL, BECAUSE EACH TYPE CAN BE FOUND IN DIFFERENT WAYS. FOR EXAMPLE, ARTICLES WILL BE FOUND IN A SPECIFIC VOLUME AND ISSUE OF A PERIODICAL, BUT A BOOK STANDS ON ITS OWN.

STILL, REGARDLESS OF STYLE OR ITEM TYPE, YOU'LL NEED SIMILAR INFORMATION TO HELP READERS LOCATE THE UNIQUE RESOURCE.

LET'S SAY WE WANT TO CREATE A CITATION FOR A JOURNAL ARTICLE IN APA STYLE.

I'LL JUST PUSH THESE AND...

WHIRRRRRR

CLICK

...UH-OH.

Author Last Name, Author Initials. (Year of publication). Article title. Title of Journal, volume number (issue number), pages.

http://dx.doi.org/xx.xxx/yyyyy

WELL, I MADE A MESS, BUT WE'VE GOT WHAT WE NEED HERE. THE APA STRUCTURE FOR A JOURNAL ARTICLE CITATION.*

*SEE "Research and Citation Resources" by Purdue OWL (https://owl.purdue.edu/owl/research_and_citation/resources.html) FOR MORE DETAILS AND TIPS.

HERE'S WHAT HAPPENS WHEN WE REPLACE THE EXAMPLE WITH SOME REAL INFO.

Manningham, P. (2014). I've lost the remote in my couch and *Dancing with the Stars* is on: A case study in apathy and decision-making. *Journal for Lazy Scientists, 37*(2), 38–50.

EVERY STYLE HAS ITS QUIRKS. APA DOESN'T WANT YOU TO CAPITALIZE THE WORDS IN THE JOURNAL ARTICLE TITLE, EXCEPT FOR THE FIRST WORD, PROPER NOUNS, OR THE FIRST WORD IN A SUBTITLE. THE JOURNAL TITLE AND VOLUME NUMBER ARE IN ITALICS.

OF COURSE, BOOKS AND ARTICLES AREN'T THE ONLY SOURCES THAT NEED CITING. DEPENDING ON THE TOPIC, YOU MIGHT CITE MOVIES, DOCUMENTARIES, TV SHOWS, PODCASTS, WEBSITES...YOU NAME IT. WE LIVE IN AN AGE OF MEDIA!

EACH STYLE MANUAL HAS METHODS FOR CITING EVERYTHING FROM BLOGS TO VIDEO RECORDINGS OF LIVE MUSIC PERFORMANCES.

AND CITATIONS DON'T ALWAYS HAVE TO BE "OFFICIAL." WHEN YOU PROVIDE A LINK ONLINE, THAT'S A SIMPLE, INFORMAL, AND EASY WAY TO CITE A SOURCE. REMEMBER, IT'S ALL ABOUT LETTING YOUR AUDIENCE KNOW THAT YOU'VE BORROWED SOME INFORMATION AND THAT YOU'RE ABLE TO EXPLAIN WHERE YOU GOT IT FROM.

"Climate gentrification" is hurting low-income families as sea levels rise. http://sitn.hms.harvard.edu/flash/2019/climate-newest-gentrifying-force-effects-already-re-shaping-cities/

THAT DOESN'T MEAN YOU CAN'T MAKE LIMITED USE OF COPYRIGHTED MATERIAL, THOUGH. IN SCHOLARLY WRITING, YOU **HAVE** TO! WHEN YOU CITE SOMEONE ELSE'S WORK TO SUPPORT YOUR OWN, THAT'S BASICALLY WHAT YOU'RE DOING. AND YOU'RE TRANSFORMING IT INTO SOMETHING NEW... AN ORIGINAL PIECE OF SCHOLARSHIP.

DONE PROPERLY, CITATION IS NOT A BREACH OF COPYRIGHT. IF YOU USE ONLY SMALL PIECES OF A WORK AND GIVE PROPER ATTRIBUTION TO ITS AUTHOR, IT'S GENERALLY PERMISSIBLE.

KEEP IN MIND WE'RE TALKING STRICTLY SCHOLARLY, NONPROFIT USE HERE. IF YOU'RE PLANNING ON RELEASING A SAMPLE-HEAVY SONG ANYTIME SOON, YOU MIGHT WANT TO LAWYER UP, JUST IN CASE.

IF YOU'RE WRITING RESEARCH PAPERS, THOUGH, IT'S ALL GOOD. JUST FOLLOW THE RULES!

SO HOW DO YOU KNOW WHAT'S OK AND WHAT'S NOT WHEN IT COMES TO COPYRIGHT? THE KEY IS TO UNDERSTAND THE CONCEPT OF FAIR USE.

IN UNITED STATES COPYRIGHT LAW, THE FAIR USE DOCTRINE* DESCRIBES ACCEPTABLE USES OF COPYRIGHTED MATERIAL.

*17 U.S.C. §107 (FOR THOSE WHO DON'T SPEAK LEGALESE, THAT MEANS "SECTION 107 OF TITLE 17 OF THE UNITED STATES CODE"). SEE "Copyright Law of the United States" (https://www.copyright.gov/title17/).

CHAPTER SEVEN

WHAT IS

...the purpose and character of the use? Commercial? Nonprofit and/or educational?

...the nature of the copyrighted work?

...the amount (significance) of the portion used in relation to the copyrighted work as a whole?

...the effect of the use upon the potential market for, or value of, the copyrighted work?

THE LAW DOESN'T EXACTLY DEFINE WHAT'S ALLOWED WITH COPYRIGHTED MATERIAL—AND OBVIOUSLY THIS IS TOO BIG A TOPIC TO EXPLORE HERE—BUT IT DOES ESTABLISH FOUR CRITERIA USED TO DETERMINE WHETHER OR NOT AN APPROPRIATION IS FAIR USE.

THESE FACTORS ARE YOUR GUIDE.

AS A GENERAL RULE, FAIR USE REQUIRES THAT YOUR WORK DOESN'T DAMAGE THE ORIGINAL WORK'S COMMERCIAL POTENTIAL AND USES ONLY A SMALL PERCENTAGE OF THE ORIGINAL WORK.

NOT EVERY USE OF COPYRIGHTED MATERIAL MUST BE NONPROFIT OR EDUCATIONAL, SO LONG AS THE END PRODUCT IS SUBSTANTIVELY DIFFERENT FROM THE ORIGINAL WORK IN QUESTION, BUT COPYRIGHT LAW DOESN'T DEFINE **ANY** OF THIS STUFF IN CONCRETE TERMS...WHICH IS WHY NON-SCHOLARLY USE OF COPYRIGHTED MATERIAL IS BEST LEFT TO EXPERTS.

OR PEOPLE WHO CAN AFFORD TO **HIRE** EXPERTS.

THIS ARTIST SAMPLES SO MUCH, SHE'S GOING TO END UP PAYING FOR MY SUMMER HOME.

PLAY IT SAFE. WHEN IT COMES TO COPYRIGHT, ERR ON THE SIDE OF CAUTION!

SOME CORPORATIONS FIGHT EVERY USE OF THEIR INTELLECTUAL PROPERTY, EVEN FAIR USE. THESE COMPANIES HAVE DEEP POCKETS AND ARMIES OF LAWYERS.

WE HEAR YOU'VE PAINTED SOME CARTOON CHARACTERS ON YOUR WALL. HERE'S A SUBPOENA.

DAY CARE

THEY CAN BE OVERZEALOUS IN ASSERTING THEIR RIGHTS, AND THAT'S HOW COPYRIGHT GOT A BAD NAME IN CERTAIN CIRCLES AND WHY MANY ACTIVELY OPPOSE TRADITIONAL COPYRIGHT.*

THIS MAY NOT OFTEN AFFECT YOUR ACADEMIC WORK, BUT IT'S WORTH BEING AWARE OF.

*MANY OF THESE CASES HAVE MORE TO DO WITH TRADEMARK THAN COPYRIGHT, BUT THAT'S ANOTHER SUBJECT ENTIRELY.

*SEE creativecommons.org FOR MORE INFORMATION!

CHAPTER SEVEN

Attribution (CC BY)

THIS LICENSE ALLOWS REUSERS TO DISTRIBUTE, REMIX, ADAPT, AND BUILD UPON THE MATERIAL IN ANY MEDIUM OR FORMAT, SO LONG AS ATTRIBUTION IS GIVEN TO THE CREATOR. THE LICENSE ALLOWS FOR COMMERCIAL USE.

Attribution ShareAlike (CC BY-SA)

THIS LICENSE ALLOWS REUSERS TO DISTRIBUTE, REMIX, ADAPT, AND BUILD UPON THE MATERIAL IN ANY MEDIUM OR FORMAT, SO LONG AS ATTRIBUTION IS GIVEN TO THE CREATOR. THE LICENSE ALLOWS FOR COMMERCIAL USE. IF YOU REMIX, ADAPT, OR BUILD UPON THE MATERIAL, YOU MUST LICENSE THE MODIFIED MATERIAL UNDER IDENTICAL TERMS.

Attribution-NonCommercial (CC BY-NC)

THIS LICENSE ALLOWS REUSERS TO DISTRIBUTE, REMIX, ADAPT, AND BUILD UPON THE MATERIAL IN ANY MEDIUM OR FORMAT FOR NONCOMMERCIAL PURPOSES ONLY, AND ONLY SO LONG AS ATTRIBUTION IS GIVEN TO THE CREATOR.

Attribution-NonCommercial-ShareAlike (CC BY-NC-SA)

THIS LICENSE ALLOWS REUSERS TO DISTRIBUTE, REMIX, ADAPT, AND BUILD UPON THE MATERIAL IN ANY MEDIUM OR FORMAT FOR NONCOMMERCIAL PURPOSES ONLY, AND ONLY SO LONG AS ATTRIBUTION IS GIVEN TO THE CREATOR. IF YOU REMIX, ADAPT, OR BUILD UPON THE MATERIAL, YOU MUST LICENSE THE MODIFIED MATERIAL UNDER IDENTICAL TERMS.

Attribution-NoDerivatives (CC BY-ND)

THIS LICENSE ALLOWS REUSERS TO COPY AND DISTRIBUTE THE MATERIAL IN ANY MEDIUM OR FORMAT IN UNADAPTED FORM ONLY, AND ONLY SO LONG AS ATTRIBUTION IS GIVEN TO THE CREATOR. THE LICENSE ALLOWS FOR COMMERCIAL USE.

Attribution-NonCommercial-NoDerivatives (CC BY-NC-ND)

THIS LICENSE ALLOWS REUSERS TO COPY AND DISTRIBUTE THE MATERIAL IN ANY MEDIUM OR FORMAT IN UNADAPTED FORM ONLY, FOR NONCOMMERCIAL PURPOSES ONLY, AND ONLY SO LONG AS ATTRIBUTION IS GIVEN TO THE CREATOR.

Public Domain (CC Zero)

THIS LICENSE IS A PUBLIC DEDICATION TOOL, WHICH ALLOWS CREATORS TO GIVE UP THEIR COPYRIGHT AND PUT THEIR WORKS INTO THE WORLDWIDE PUBLIC DOMAIN. CCO ALLOWS REUSERS TO DISTRIBUTE, REMIX, ADAPT, AND BUILD UPON THE MATERIAL IN ANY MEDIUM OR FORMAT, WITH NO CONDITIONS.

SEE, THIS IS HOW YOU DO IT!

YOU CAN FIND CC LICENSED WORK USING CCSEARCH AT https://search.creativecommons.org/.

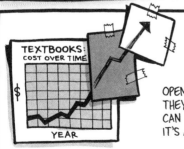

TEXTBOOKS: COST OVER TIME

$

YEAR

PEOPLE ARE DOING AMAZING THINGS WITH CC LICENSES, INCLUDING ONE OF OUR PERSONAL FAVORITES, **OPEN TEXTBOOKS**! YOU PROBABLY KNOW HOW EXPENSIVE MANY TEXTBOOKS CAN BE, AND THEY CAN ADD UP TO HUNDREDS (EVEN THOUSANDS) OF DOLLARS PER SEMESTER.

OPEN TEXTBOOKS **AREN'T JUST FREE**. SINCE THEY USE CC LICENSING, THEY CAN BE ADAPTED AND REMIXED, AND STUDENTS AND TEACHERS CAN WORK TOGETHER ON CREATING NEW CONTENT FOR COURSES. IT'S A GREAT WAY TO SHARE THE CREATIVE SPIRIT OF EDUCATION.

CHECK OUT THE OPEN TEXTBOOK LIBRARY (https://open.umn.edu/opentextbooks) FOR HUNDREDS OF EXAMPLES OF TEXTBOOKS, AND BE SURE TO SHARE WITH YOUR PROFESSORS AND LIBRARIANS.

CRITICAL THINKING EXERCISES

1. What aspects of plagiarism and citation concern you the most? Are there areas that are not clear, or are you very confident in your skills and experience? Explain.

2. Practice paraphrasing and summarizing information from your sources. Be sure to use the appropriate in-text citation method to note where you got the idea from. Need help? Use an online resource like Purdue OWL, Citation Fox, Google Scholar, or the appropriate style manual (APA, MLA, Chicago, etc.).

3. Review the various Creative Commons licenses at https://creativecommons.org/about/cclicenses/. What advantages/disadvantages does each license have for the creator and those who use the work?

4. Visit the Open Textbook Library at https://open.umn.edu/opentextbooks. Search for text-books in a subject for a class you are currently taking. How many did you find? Choose one to examine in more detail and skim the chapter titles, introduction, and index. How does it compare to the current textbook for that class? What are some advantages and disadvantages of using an open textbook?

CONCLUSION

THERE YOU HAVE IT, FOLKS. A CRASH COURSE IN BASIC INFORMATION LITERACY AND RESEARCH, FROM CREATING THESIS STATEMENTS TO PROPER SEARCHING THROUGH DIFFERENT KINDS OF INFORMATION SOURCES...

AND CITATION! DON'T FORGET CITATION.

TRUTH BE TOLD, WE COULD HAVE FILLED A BOOK THIS SIZE WITH TIPS AND TECHNIQUES FOR ANY **ONE** OF THE SUBJECTS WE'VE COVERED. BEING INFORMATION LITERATE IS A SKILL SET, SURE, BUT IT'S ALSO A WAY TO APPROACH THINKING ABOUT AND UNDERSTANDING INFORMATION.

IT'S A SCIENCE AND AN ART, NOW THAT I THINK ABOUT IT.

THE THING ABOUT INFORMATION LITERACY IS THAT YOU'RE ALWAYS GOING TO BE WORKING AT IT. IT'S AN ONGOING PROCESS. INFORMATION WILL CHANGE AND EXPAND, AND YOU'LL HAVE TO ADJUST TO KEEP UP. **SO**, NEVER STOP PRACTICING. REMEMBER TO THINK CAREFULLY ABOUT YOUR INFORMATION NEEDS, BE A PART OF ONGOING SCHOLARLY CONVERSATIONS, PARTICIPATE ETHICALLY, AND BE WILLING TO EXPLORE INFORMATION OUTSIDE YOUR COMFORT ZONE. AND DO ALL THIS WITH A HEALTHY MEASURE OF SKEPTICISM REGARDING INFORMATION AND THOSE WHO PRODUCE IT. IT SOUNDS LIKE A LOT, BUT IT JUST TAKES PRACTICE.

IT'S TRUE. EXPLAINING THIS STUFF MAKES IT SOUND HARDER THAN IT ACTUALLY IS! YOU'LL REALIZE THAT ONCE YOU'RE IN YOUR GROOVE.

"IN YOUR GROOVE"?

YOU HEARD ME.

BEST OF LUCK TO YOU ALL! STUDY HARD, CITE RIGHT, AND REMEMBER, AS LONG AS YOU'VE GOT THIS BOOK...

CONCLUSION

CRITICAL THINKING EXERCISES

1. Review your blog/website/etc. How has your understanding changed from your first posts to now?

2. How has your own past ignorance of information literacy affected the quality of your academic work? How will your current knowledge improve it?

3. If you had to teach information literacy concepts to someone else, what would you emphasize and why?

ACKNOWLEDGMENTS

We would like to thank a number of people who have provided support and guidance through-out this revision project. Our editors, Mary Laur and Mollie McFee, rekindled our interest in revising the book and offered their expert advice on how to say more with less in order to let the fantastic artwork of Kevin Cannon shine. We have no doubt that Kevin's work is what draws students in and makes these concepts come alive. Thanks to Mike Hall for his friend-ship, his ideas, and the great fun Matt had while collaborating with him on library comics for just about a decade. Thank you all for contributing to this collaborative effort.

We thank our colleagues at Oklahoma State University for helping shape our approach to information literacy instruction. We have all grown as educators over the past five years, and we hope that this book successfully implements the lessons we've learned together. Thanks, in particular, to Cristina Colquhoun, a wonderful instructional designer and friend who prior-itizes student learning and well-being above all else.

There have been many researchers and practitioners whose work has guided us in our instruction and in this book. We note some of them throughout the work, especially Dr. Safiya Umoja Noble and Mike Caulfield, but we also want to acknowledge the many librarians who have worked on building a greater understanding of critical information literacy in the profes-sion. Without their contributions, we'd still be doing the same old things in the same old way.

Thanks to the librarians, instructors, and students who use this book. We hope it will en-courage you to seek out ways to challenge systems of oppression and fight for more equitable avenues to information creation and access.

Above all, we thank our families for their patience and love. Matt thanks Irene, Colin (who successfully did not care about this project either time), and Nate (who, last time, was thanked before we even knew what we'd name him). Holly is not as witty as Matt, but nonetheless thanks her husband Tony and her parents, Mary and Leonard.

GLOSSARY

abstract. A brief summary of a research article that explains the context and importance of the study.

advanced searching. Many databases and search engines offer advanced search options that allow you to make searching more effective and precise. These options, which can vary by resource, might allow you to search by keyword, subject, author, title, document type, etc. You may also be able to include Boolean operators (**AND, OR, NOT**) using a drop-down menu within an advanced search.

algorithmic bias. Characteristics of a computer program that lead to unfair discrimination against individuals or groups of people.

author search. A type of advanced search that allows you to search for resources by the name of the author. Traditionally, it is best to perform an author search by listing the last name of the author followed by a comma and then the author's first name, if necessary, although the comma is increasingly unnecessary in more and more library resources. Example: Smith, Earl

bibliography. May also be known as works cited or references (although they are technically different, they serve the same purpose), depending on the writing style you are using (APA, MLA, and Chicago are common examples of style). Basically, a bibliography lists the sources that an author has utilized in the research and writing of a paper, article, or book. This list provides a way for others to find, examine, and verify the information that was used in the research. A good existing bibliography can help you get your own research started. If you find a good source, check its bibliography for other potential sources for your own research.

Boolean operators. AND, **OR**, and **NOT** are known as Boolean operators within online library databases and search engines. You can use these terms to "connect" your search terms and appropriately narrow or broaden your search for information. **AND** can be used to narrow a search. For example, a search for "obesity **AND** children" would help you find materials that address both of those terms. **OR** is used to broaden a search and is useful when you are dealing with terms that might be interchangeable. A good example of this is a search for "teens **OR** adolescents." **NOT** is used to limit a search by eliminating a specific term from your results. You could use a search for "immigration law **NOT** United States" to help you find information on immigration law outside the United States. You can also use multiple operators within a search, either in the search bar using parentheses or with advanced searching options. A more complex search might look like this: "(birth control **OR** contraception) **AND** (United States **OR** Europe)."

citation. The process of explaining where you found the information you're using in your research. This includes the use of in-text citations, footnotes, or endnotes to indicate when you've used information from a specific source, as well as the full reference included in the bibliography/works cited/references that notes details such as the author, title, date, and other identifying information for a source.

citation styles. Various organizations have developed particular writing styles for different academic disciplines and purposes. Common examples of styles are APA (American Psychological Association), MLA (Modern Language Association), and Chicago style. These styles differ in many aspects, but one of the most obvious and important ways is how sources are cited. Although the information included in the citations can be very similar, the order of the information, as well as punctuation, capitalization, and the actual in-text citation/footnote/endnote will vary. For more information, check the appropriate style manual or use a reliable online resource like Purdue's Online Writing Lab (OWL).

classification. Refers to the various systems used to organize and locate physical resources within a library. Common systems used in the United States include the Dewey Decimal system and the Library of Congress system. Essentially, classification helps keep similar items grouped together, which can allow for more efficient access to materials. These two systems break down information into broad subjects, with more and more narrow ranges of information fitting within each broad range. Items are often assigned a call number based on where they fall within the classification system. These call numbers are used to place items in a specific order so that they can be located later, usually by locating the call number within the **library search**.

controlled vocabulary. A way to provide a standardized and single term that can be used in the place of similar terms, especially in the case of library searches and databases. For example, the term "automobile" may be used in the place of "car," "truck," "van," etc. Controlled vocabularies make searching a less chaotic process by assigning identical terms to resources that cover similar material. **Subject headings** are a type of controlled vocabulary.

database. Simply put, a database is a collection of information that is organized and searchable. One type of database lets you search through print and electronic materials in the library. In the **information literacy** context, the term "database" usually refers to a library resource that can be used to locate digital articles in academic journals, newspapers, magazines, and other resources. Databases, unlike many library searches, let you search within a journal title for a specific article.

Dewey Decimal classification. *See* classification.

discovery search. *See* library search.

disinformation. *See* misinformation.

faceted searching. This is a way to refine or limit your list of search results, much like you can do when shopping online. For example, you might be searching for a tent to purchase. You search the store for "tent" and then notice that you can narrow your search by the brand or capacity. You can often find the same kind of tools within a library search or database, except you can limit your search results by subject, format, location, date of publication, and many other variables. This approach gives you the freedom to enter your own search terms and then narrow down your results in a very controlled manner.

Google. Just google it.

Google Scholar. An open web search engine from Google that contains information about scholarly articles, books, and case law but does not always provide full-text access to these resources.

information literacy. The ability to find, access, understand, and use information ethically for specific needs.

information overload. We all deal with an insane amount of information. Sometimes it can be too difficult to manage, especially when you are trying to do research and just don't know how to find the right information floating out there in the middle of all the wrong information. That's information overload, and you can help prevent it by knowing how to best utilize library and web resources, as well as understanding how to evaluate and use the information that you are able to locate through those resources.

journals (academic/peer-reviewed/scholarly). Academic journals are periodical publications that can be found in print or online and offer the most up-to-date research on a given topic. They're like magazines written by and for professors and researchers. Research is usually reviewed by other professionals before it is published to make sure the information is correct (*see* **peer review**). There are thousands and thousands of journals out there, so there are probably many that address your research topic. Typically, your best bet for accessing journals in your library is through a database, although many libraries still carry hard copies.

keyword searching. Usually, the generic default search option in a library search or database. Keywords can potentially be found anywhere in a **record** or the full text of an item, so this type of search may not be very useful unless you use multiple keywords connected with **Boolean operators**.

Library of Congress classification. *See* classification.

library search. A system that allows a user to search both a library's print collection and at least some electronic resources, which may include databases, journals, videos, and more.

metadata. When discussing library tools like searches and databases, metadata can be understood as descriptive information about the items within those searches and databases. Metadata might describe the author, title, subject, and contents of a book, as well as its physical dimensions, call number, format type, and many other traits. Although the actual metadata **record** looks complicated, it is presented to you, the library patron, in a very simple format. When you view the details of an item in a search or database, you are viewing a "cleaned-up" version of the metadata. Metadata makes searching easier by providing a structure to the way that the descriptive information is recorded, organized, and searched. When you perform a search, it is the metadata that is being examined.

misinformation/disinformation. False information that is shared, sometimes unintentionally, but often purposely with the intent to deceive.

open access. Information, usually research and scholarly articles, that is freely available online for anyone to access and may be licensed for people to use, share, and adapt, with some limitations.

open educational resources. Resources for teaching and learning purposes that are licensed for people to freely use and share, and may sometimes include a license to adapt. This also includes materials that are in the public domain.

peer review. This refers to the process that academic/scholarly journal articles (and other publications) go through to help ensure that the research is accurate, reliable, and up-to-date before it is published. Basically, an author submits their article to a journal where an editor decides if the article will be considered for publication. If so, the article is sent out to be read and reviewed by other professionals in the field who help determine if the work is accurate and if it makes a new contribution to existing research on that topic. The reviewers may suggest edits and the author will consider revising the article before the editor makes a final decision about whether to publish it or not.

periodicals. Unlike books, periodicals (such as newspapers, magazines, and academic journals) are continually published on a schedule (daily, weekly, monthly, etc.) with new content in every "issue." The traditional idea of periodicals is changing with technology. Websites can update information on a minute-to-minute basis without having to worry about publishing a physical item. Still, even though many academic journals and popular periodicals can use the web to stay current and offer updates, they may continue to release articles and other materials that require review or editing on a scheduled basis. More and more often, you will be likely to access periodical articles (especially from academic journals) through your library **databases**.

professional/trade journal. A publication written for professionals and practitioners in a particular industry.

record. In a library search or database, the record refers to the information that describes an item or resource. You usually encounter a record after you click on a link to a specific item in the search or database. The record includes information like author, title, publisher, subject headings, contents, call number, journal title, volume, and issue (as applicable). This information is part of the **metadata** that is used to describe the item.

references. *See* bibliography.

research. Refers to the process of developing a research topic, establishing a question or a thesis statement, and then collecting appropriate information from various resources in order to address that question. It is about knowing how to locate the right information using the right tools in the right way. Of course, there are different types of research. Library research doesn't require you to wear a lab coat and laugh maniacally, although that might help to clear a study space in the library.

search engine. Google, DuckDuckGo, and Bing are examples of popular search engines that are used to search the web for information. Search engines work by sending "spiders" or "crawlers" out into the web to bring back information from all the websites they can visit. Copies of web pages are stored by each search engine and are combed through when you perform a search. Each search engine is different and may give you different results for identical searches. Search engines have advanced search options, but they differ somewhat from those found in library searches and databases since the **metadata** for websites is different than for library resources.

search statement. When searching in a **library search** or **database** or when using a web **search engine**, a search statement refers to what you put in the search bar. It is best to create a search statement using good terms or keywords drawn from your research question or topic and connect them with **Boolean operators** to ensure good search results. For example, if your topic is the effects of pets on elderly health, your search statement might be "pets **AND** elderly **AND** health" or maybe just "pets **AND** elderly." You want to make sure that you eliminate the "fluff" from your search statements and include the essential terms.

search terms. *See* search statement.

spiders/crawlers. *See* search engine.

subject headings/subject terms. These are a type of **controlled vocabulary** used to describe what a resource is about. Subject terms are more specific than keywords since a keyword can be found anywhere within a record. A subject term or heading is a specific part of the **metadata** and can be searched separately (much like a title or an author search). In many library searches and databases, a subject term or thesaurus search (a type of **advanced searching** technique) will result not in a list of items, but a list of relevant subjects and subdivisions that can then be used to locate items that fit that specific subject heading. For example, you might perform a subject term or thesaurus search in a database for "environmental policy." The results might include a broad subject heading for "environmental policy" that would lead to many articles on the subject, but you could also look at the subdivisions for the subject, which lead to resources on the health and ethical aspects of environmental policy. The articles under those specific subheadings would be narrower and perhaps more appropriate to your topic.

subject searching. *See* subject headings.

title search. An **advanced search** option used to search for items by their title. A title search specifically looks at the part of the **metadata** record that deals with the title of the item.

truncation. *See* wildcard.

Wikipedia. A web encyclopedia that can potentially be edited by anyone. *Wikipedia* can be an excellent starting point for your research and can help you get a very basic idea of a topic, as well as guide you toward other, more scholarly resources. Remember that the information from a *Wikipedia* article came from somewhere, so you should go to the original source if you want to use the information in your own research. It's not generally advisable to use and cite *Wikipedia* in your academic research, unless of course you are researching *Wikipedia*!

wildcard. An **advanced searching** option used to help you find resources that may use an alternate spelling or variation of a search term. Library searches and databases often offer multiple wildcard options, sometimes allowing a special character to stand in for other characters. Truncation is an example of a wildcard option. Although each database or library search may use a different symbol to indicate truncation, an asterisk is often used. Example: a search for "theor*" would result in resources including "theory," "theoretical," "theorist," etc.

works cited. *See* bibliography.